God in Pain

Other Titles in the
Teaching Sermon Series

THE TEACHING SERMON SERIES

Ronald J. Allen, Editor

God in Pain

Teaching Sermons on Suffering

BARBARA BROWN TAYLOR

Abingdon Press
Nashville

GOD IN PAIN:
TEACHING SERMONS ON SUFFERING

Copyright © 1998 by Barbara Brown Taylor

All rights reserved.

This book is printed on recycled, acid-free, elemental-chlorine–free paper.

Library of Congress Cataloging-in-Publication Data

Taylor, Barbara Brown.
  God in pain : teaching sermons on suffering / Barbara Brown Taylor.
    p. cm.— (The teaching sermon series)
  Includes bibliographical references.
  ISBN 0-687-05887-2 (alk. paper)
  1. Pain—Religious aspects—Christianity—Sermons. 2. Teaching sermons.
3. Sermons, American. 4. Episcopal Church—Sermons.
I. Title. II. Series.
BT732.7.T37 1998
248.8'6—dc21
                                     97-44059
                                          CIP

Scripture quotations, unless otherwise indicated, are from the New Revised Standard Version Bible, copyright © 1989, by the Division of Christian Education of the National Council of the Churches of Christ in the United States of America.

Scripture quotations noted NEB are from The New English Bible. © The Delegates of the Oxford University Press and The Syndics of the Cambridge University Press 1961, 1970. Reprinted by permission.

Chapter 2, "A Cure for Despair," was published in *The Journal for Preachers*, Advent 1997.

06 07 — 10 9

MANUFACTURED IN THE UNITED STATES OF AMERICA

Contents

PART II
PAIN OF DEATH

EPILOGUE
PREACHING CHRIST CRUCIFIED

Foreword

DYNAMIC TEACHING OF THE CHRISTIAN FAITH BUILDS STRONG congregations that make a vital witness. Faithful Christian teaching helps the Christian community respond to the two most important questions in life. Who are we in the light of the gospel? What does the gospel call us to do? The Teaching Sermon Series aims to provide examples of effective teaching sermons.

The time is ripe for a focus on the teaching ministry of the pulpit. Teaching is a prominent emphasis in the preaching of many congregations that are growing in size, in depth of Christian commitment, and in outreach. Teaching sermons appeal to many people today. Further, many contemporary congregations (particularly in the old-line denominations) are declining because they do not have a distinctive sense of Christian identity and mission or a sufficient flow of spiritual energy. Teaching sermons invite diminished churches to the new life that can come when the resources of the gospel, the Bible, Christian tradition, and doctrine are integrated into everyday Christian experience.

The people of God are by nature a teaching community, as Deuteronomy makes clear: "Hear, O Israel: The LORD is our God, the LORD alone. . . . Recite [these words] to your children and talk about them when you are at home and when you are away, when you lie down and when you rise" (Deuteronomy 6:4-7). Teaching is constitutive of the identity of the leaders of the people of God as we recognize by recalling the teaching dimensions of some of the formative ministries of our tradition: Moses, Deborah, Ezra, Jesus, Paul, Priscilla, Origen, Augustine, Catherine of Siena, Luther, Calvin, Wesley, King, Malcolm, McFague, Dozier, Suchocki. A great cloud of witnesses empowers the pastor who would teach from the pulpit.

Teaching sermons have their best effect when they are part of a systemic approach to teaching Christian faith that permeates the Christian community. In the congregational setting, the sermon can play key roles in helping a community develop a consciousness for learning. First, the sermon can be a significant moment of teaching and learning in its own right. The service of worship is the largest regular gathering of the congregation. In a single moment, the preacher has the opportunity to touch the heart, mind, and will of the community. Second, by modeling the vitalization that results from Christian teaching, the sermon can encourage the members of the congregation to take part in the smaller learning groups that are a part of the congregation's life. Third, the sermon can sensitize the congregation to the ways in which the gospel is taught (or not taught) in all that happens in the life of the church.

As I point out in an earlier book, *The Teaching Sermon* (Nashville: Abingdon Press, 1995), there is no single format for teaching sermons. Teaching and learning can take place in multiple ways. Some educational sermons are linear in sequence and informational in tone, while others are associative and evocative. Many teaching sermons combine sequential and associative patterns, as well as analytical and aesthetic approaches. Some teaching sermons center on biblical texts or themes, while others give an interpretation of Christian doctrine, while still others help the congregation reflect on contemporary theological and moral issues. The subjects and methods of Christian teaching are as varied as life itself. The Teaching Sermon Series illustrates the variety in both style and content that is possible when the preacher is a teacher.

Ronald J. Allen

THIS PAST CHRISTMAS, I SAT DOWN WITH MY FOUR-YEAR-OLD goddaughter Madeline to look at her new story Bible. She began by showing me her favorite pictures, which were Adam and Eve hiding from God in the garden of Eden and Absalom hanging from a tree by his hair. As she outlined the story of the flood for me, my fingers began to itch. I wanted to see how the authors of this children's book had presented Jesus' death. Could I look ahead, I asked her? "This is not about Jesus yet," she said sternly, but she let me look anyway.

I had to look hard. In between a long account of the last supper and a richly illustrated section on the empty tomb, I found half a page with a picture of three crosses far away on a hillside at sunset. It was so small and dark that I could not even tell whether the crosses were occupied. The text was not much help. "Then Jesus was put to death," it read, "but he did not stay dead for long. God had planned a big surprise for him, which happened at dawn on Easter morning."

That is all Madeline will learn about the suffering of Christ (from that book at least). The authors apparently decided that God's pain would be too hard for a child to understand. So they left it out, and I imagine that more than a few parents are grateful to them. Who wants to explain that bloody episode to a child? Who can say why God let it happen without prompting even harder questions? "But I thought you said God *loved* Jesus."

Children are not the only ones who have trouble with God's pain. Like them, many of us assume that anyone with the power to avoid pain would do so, which makes the death of the Messiah as much a scandal now as it ever was. Paul taught us to understand it as atonement, within a frame of human guilt and divine judgment. Luther saw it as Christ's greatest act of identification with frail flesh. Some contemporary theologians have accused God of child abuse. The homiletical issue is how to remain faithful to the whole paradoxical story without falling off either side of it; that is, without proclaiming either a punishing God or one who simply does not care.

The irony is that we need a God who knows about pain. Anyone who has suffered through even one night of deep hurt knows what it is to beg for relief. Sometimes the prayer is answered and sometimes it is not, but those who have been there will often say that the strange, sweet presence of Christ in their suffering becomes dearer to them than the hope of recovery.

To speak of God in pain, then, is not only to address the biblical stories of Christ's suffering and death but also to proclaim the God who is present in our pain. As much as we might like to limit that part of our lives to half a page, it looms larger than that for most of us, and the preacher who will not talk about our collisions with betrayal, dread, or despair is a preacher who does not want to know very much about us. One who will—who will even dare to look for the good news in pain—may do more to heal us than the finest physician.

This volume of sermons practices different approaches to the problem of God's presence in pain. First, a section on the ordinary pain of human life on earth, followed by a section on the exquisite pain of Good Friday, and finally, an epilogue for all of us who presume to preach Christ crucified. All these sermons are presumptuous, insofar as no one can say for sure what God meant by the cross. Still, it is there for us to look at—either far away on a hillside at sunset or so close up that we have to cover one eye. It would be a mistake for us to cover them both, for then we should miss something very, very important that God has gone to great lengths to show us.

Because these sermons are part of a teaching series, let me add a word about method. Mine is largely intuitive, starting out with a whole assortment of ideas, images, and phrases that have emerged from the text and then juggling them until only the best remain in the air. By "the best," I mean those that are moving, interesting, tactile, and true to human experience. Also those that matter. Every Sunday I preach to at least three people who are dying of something. My general rule of thumb is this: any sermon I preach has to be worth the time they are giving to it. They may be the only ones in the house who know that hearing the gospel is a matter of life or death, but that makes them the best listeners we have.

I work under the assumption that the development of an image is as important as the development of an idea—more important, perhaps—since there is every reason to believe that conversion is an imaginative process and not an intellectual one. When people discover new life, it is often a matter of trading in their old images for new ones, so that they see themselves, their neighbors, and the whole story of life on earth in a different way. The development of imagery in a sermon can work out in the open, with full comment on the images under revision, but it works even better out of view, like a bass line that carries the tune without anyone even being aware of it.

I also work under the assumption that words matter, and that choosing the right one is the difference between a sentence that works and one that does not. Scripture is full of words whose power is their beauty. God would never say "food" if "manna" or "milk and honey" were possibilities.

Lectionary preachers will understand why all the sermons in part 2 are based on the Gospel of John. The set reading for Good Friday is John 18:1–19:42, and each of these sermons begins with that full narrative still ringing in the ear.

In closing, I want to thank Ron Allen for inviting me to take part in this project, and Judith Barber, director of the Hambidge Center in Rabun Gap, Georgia, for the residency that allowed me to complete this project. And as always, my thanks to my husband, Ed, who is my best coach and main support.

Barbara Brown Taylor
Clarkesville, Georgia
Pentecost 1997

PART I

Pain of Life

Chapter One

The Gift of Disillusionment

Matthew 11:2-11

"ARE YOU THE ONE WHO IS TO COME, OR are we to wait for another?" That has to be one of the most haunting questions in all of scripture, especially when you consider who is asking it. It is John speaking through his disciples—John the Baptist, who has devoted his life to preparing the way of the Lord and making his paths straight. John, who was standing waist deep in the River Jordan when he looked up, saw Jesus, and tried to change places with him. "I need to be baptized by you," he said, "and do you come to me?" John, who was there when the heavens opened and the spirit of God descended like a dove, lighting on Jesus as a voice from heaven proclaimed who he was for all to hear. "This is my beloved Son, with whom I am well pleased."

"Are you the one who is to come, or are we to wait for another?" What in the world has happened to John that he should ask such a thing? Has his memory been erased? Has someone brainwashed him? What has made him question the identity of the one person for whom he has waited all his life?

> What in the world has happened to John that he should ask such a thing?

Well, he is in jail, for one thing, put there by Herod not for preaching on street corners but for disapproving of Herod's marriage to his brother's wife. It will not be long before Herod's new step-daughter asks for John's head on a silver platter, but meanwhile nothing has gone the way John thought it would.

The Messiah was supposed to change things. He was supposed to burn up all the human trash and dead wood of the world. He was supposed to come with a sharp ax, with a gleaming pitchfork, and separate the good guys from the bad guys once and for all. He was supposed to clean up the world, so that people like Herod were no longer in power and people like John were no longer in prison, but Jesus has utterly failed to meet John's expectations.

He talks more about peace and love than he does about sin and hell. He spends most of his time with spiritual weaklings and moral misfits, and he does precious little to chop up the rotten wood that John has singled out for fiery destruction. Jesus seems more inter-ested in poking around the dead stumps looking for new growth and in throwing parties for the new shoots when he finds them, and all in all it is more than John can bear.

"Are you the one who is to come, or are we to wait for another?" This is John's Calvary, his moment of wondering what his life has been about and fearing that there has been a terrible mistake. It is his moment of wondering if he has been forsaken, if the one for whom he has waited all this time has turned out to be an imposter—not the Messiah at all, but an idealistic dreamer whom the world will swat down as easily as a gnat.

> *This is John's Calvary, his moment of wondering what his life has been about and fearing that there has been a terrible mistake.*

In his fine and disturbing book, *The Last Temptation of Christ*, Nikos Kazantzakis paints a picture of Jesus and John I will never forget. It is sunrise. They are sitting high above the Jordan in the hollow of a rock, where they have been arguing all night long about what to do with the world. John's face is hard and decisive; from time to time his arms go up and down as though he were actually chopping something apart. Jesus' face, by contrast, is tame and hesitant. His eyes are full of compassion.

"Isn't love enough?" he asks John.

"No," John answers angrily. "The tree is rotten. God called me and gave me the ax, which I then placed at the roots of the tree. I did my duty. Now you do yours: Take the ax and strike!"

"If I were fire, I would burn," Jesus says. "If I were a woodcutter, I would strike; but I am a heart, and I love."[1]

It is not hard to understand what John was going through. We have all, at some time or another, looked for a Messiah who did not come the way we wanted him to come. You know what I mean. You want the Messiah to come and you want him to come *right now*. You want a clear, helpful answer to your questions. You want to be relieved of the burden of waking up day after day without knowing what you are supposed to do next. You want to put your hand under your pillow and find the answer there like a quarter from the tooth fairy, but morning after morning all you feel is the sheet.

Or you want a Messiah who will rescue the innocent and punish the guilty. Your prayers focus on the latter. You keep a long list of people who have injured you or those you love and who—according to you—do not deserve to go walking around looking and acting like normal people. You want a Messiah who will see to it that they are exposed for who they are and shunned by decent people. You have gathered a sympathetic jury, but so far you are all waiting in an empty courtroom. The judge has not shown up, and you are beginning to wonder if there is any justice in this world after all.

Or you want a Messiah who will *make* you be good. You want a Lord who will take over your mind and body so that you cannot mismanage them anymore, a Lord who will heal you in spite of yourself and who will not let you make any more mistakes. You want him to do the same thing for the whole world. One look at the news is enough to convince you that putting human beings in charge of the creation was a good idea that did not work. You will gladly surrender your freedom for a little security, and God knows the earth cannot stand much more in the way of human dominance.

But none of those is the Messiah you get. Instead, you get one who waits while you find your own answers. You get one who gives suspended sentences to the guilty. You get one who lets humankind stew in the consequences of our actions. And one day while you are moldering in your cell you send that Messiah a telegram: *"Are you the one who is to come, or are we to wait for another?"*

This is a story of crashing disillusionment—John's, ours, everyone's who looks for a Lord who does not come, or who does not come in the way he was expected—but I am here to tell you that disillusionment is not a bad thing. Disillusionment is, literally, the loss of an illusion—about ourselves, about the world, about God—and while it is almost always a painful thing, it is never a bad thing, to lose the lies we have mistaken for the truth.

Disillusioned, we find out that God does not conform to our expectations. We glimpse our own relative size in the universe and see that no human being can say who God should be or how God should act. We review our requirements of God and recognize them as our own fictions, things we tell ourselves to make ourselves feel safe or good or comfortable. Disillusioned, we find out what is not true and we are set free to seek what is—if we dare—to turn away from the God who was supposed to be in order to seek the God who is.

> *Disillusioned, we find out that God does not conform to our expectations.*

Every letdown becomes a lesson and a lure. Did God fail to come when I rubbed the lantern? Then perhaps God is not a genie. Who, then, is God? Did God fail to punish my enemies? Then perhaps God is not a cop. Who, then, is God? Did God fail to make everything run smoothly? Then perhaps God is not a mechanic. Who, then, is God?

Over and over, my disappointments draw me deeper into the mystery of God's being and doing. Every time God declines to meet my expectations, another of my idols is exposed. Another curtain is drawn back so that I can see what I have propped up in God's place. No, that is not God. Who, then, is God? It is the question of a lifetime, and the answers are never big enough or finished. Pushing past curtain after curtain, it becomes clear that the failure is not God's but my own, for having such a poor and stingy imagination.

"Go and tell John what you hear and see." That is what Jesus says to the disciples who deliver John's telegram. "The blind receive their sight, the lame walk, the lepers are cleansed, the deaf hear, the dead are raised, and the poor have good news brought to them. And blessed is anyone who takes no offense at me."

It is curious, isn't it, that he never says "I"? He never testifies to himself at all. He simply sends John's disciples back to him to tell their teacher what they have seen and heard—not a lot of wood being chopped, not a lot of fires being set—but broken people being made whole, sick people being healed, dead people being revived, and poor people being given hope.

And blessed are those who take no offense at me. Blessed are those who do not let the Messiah they are expecting blind them to the Messiah who is standing right in front of them. Blessed are those who keep a list of what God *is* doing and not only what God is *not*. Blessed are those who are not afraid to revise the hope that is in them, pushing through their disillusionment into a place of new and clearer vision.

Is he the one who is to come, or are we to wait for another? You decide. Look around you, and see. Amen.

Chapter Two

A Cure for Despair

Matthew 3:1-12

JOHN THE BAPTIST HAS ALWAYS SEEMED to me like the Doberman pinscher of the gospel. In the lectionary, he always appears right before Christmas, when no one's defenses are up. Here we are trying to get to the stable in Bethlehem. We are not hurrying. We have set a respectable pace, and with just weeks to go it really is in sight—that starlit barn where everything is about to happen. It is right up ahead there, with people already gathering around it, and for those of us who love it, it is all we can see.

We aren't thinking about the few dark blocks that still separate us from it when all of a sudden—GRRROW-ROW-ROW!!!—this big old dog with a spiky collar has got us by the ankle. "Repent, for the kingdom of heaven has come near." Before he is through, our heads are pounding with vipers, wrath, axes, and unquenchable fire, when all we really wanted was a chance to sing "O Holy Night."

And yet there is no getting around him. Every single Gospel writer introduces Jesus by talking about John, which means that in some way or another the Doberman is God's idea. John is the watchdog who makes sure no one wanders into holy precincts unaware. He is the guard dog, who tests all those who *think* they want in. Anyone who cannot handle him cannot handle the one who comes after him. As different as they will turn out to be, John's judgment precedes Jesus' grace. They go together, like night and day, because those who know nothing of judgment need nothing of grace.

> *John is the watchdog who makes sure no one wanders into holy precincts unaware.*

John's business was repentance. It was what his baptism was all about. It was not about becoming a Christian, because John was not a Christian. He had followers of his own, disciples who would become critics of the disciples of Jesus. So it is important not to confuse John's baptism with the one we know about. When John waded into the water with people, he was cleaning them up for their audience with God, which he believed would take place very soon. He begged them to change their lives in preparation for that event, and he was not below scaring them half to death if that was what it took—anything to wake them up and make them see that they were sleepwalking through their lives, most of them, confusing their own ways with God's ways and accumulating sin like an empty house accumulates dust.

He offered to hose them down, if they were willing. If they could come out of their comas long enough to see what was wrong and say so out loud, then he would wash it away for them, forever. Or God would. The same God who could make children of Abraham out of river rocks could make children of God out of them right there, if they were willing. All they had to do was consent, repent, return to the Lord, and they could start their lives all over again before they even dried off.

The past would lose its power over them. What they had done, what they had said, what they had made happen and what had happened to them would no longer run their lives. They would no longer hear those nagging voices in their heads that told them how bad they were, how ruined, and in the silence that followed they would be free to begin again, listening to God's voice this time, telling them how blessed they were, how beloved.

As scary as John was, it was a pretty great offer. No wonder people walked days to get to him. No wonder they stood around even after their turns were over, just to hear him say it again and again. "Repent, for the kingdom of heaven has come near." What sounds like a threat to us sounded like a promise to them. We hear guilt where they heard pardon, and at least part of the problem, I think, is our resistance to the whole notion of repentance.

The way most of us were taught it, repentance means owning up to how rotten you are. It means saying out loud, if only in the auditorium of your own soul, that you are a selfish, sinful, deeply defective human being who grieves the heart of God and that you are very, very sorry about it. It means dumping all your pride on the ground and stamping on it, since pride—as in ego, arrogance, vainglory—is the root of so much evil.

Only what if it isn't? What if pride isn't the problem at all, but its very opposite? What if the main thing most of us need to repent of is not our arrogance but our utter despair—that things will never change for us, that *we* will never change, that no matter what we say or do we are stuck forever in the mess we have made of our lives, or the mess someone else has made of them, but in any case that there is no hope for us, no beginning again, no chance of new life? Now *that* is a problem.

> What if the main thing most of us need to repent of is not our arrogance but our utter despair?

I cannot tell you how many people I know who are all but dead with despair. It doesn't happen just one way; it happens all kinds of ways. A little girl is abused by her grandfather and forty years later, although he is long dead and gone, his hands are still on her. She has not married. She will not let anyone get close. She is still keeping her forty-year-old promise never to let anyone hurt her like that again.

Or a family man loses his job and stays home with the kids while his wife goes to work. Their agreement is that they will change places again as soon as he finds something to do, only there are not all that many things he knows how to do. For a while he meets his goal of one interview per week, but after three months of rejections his energy just drains out of him until one afternoon his wife comes home and finds him sitting in front of the television set with an empty six-pack of Bud Dry at his feet.

Or a moody teenager doesn't know what is wrong with him, but he can't find anyone to talk to about it. His father is never home, his mother turns every talk into a sermon, and he doesn't want anyone to see him coming out of the counselor's office at school, so he starts hanging out with some people who are even moodier than he is and

that makes him feel better. When he is arrested for shoplifting a CD
at the K-Mart, no one seems all that surprised. When his mother
picks him up at the police station, she tells him he has been nothing
but trouble since the day he was born and something inside of him
that was still fluid up to that point hardens on the spot. All that
remains to be seen is just how much trouble he can be. He will try
not to let her down.

For most people, despair is a much more serious problem than
pride will ever be. It is so serious that we have a baptismal vow aimed
right at it. Q: "Will you persevere in resisting evil and, whenever you
fall into sin, repent and return to the Lord?" A: "I will, with God's
help." It is a John the Baptist vow, and it is not about keeping an eye
on our rottenness. It is about keeping an eye on our despair and never
letting it get the best of us.

Those of us who have committed ourselves to a life of repentance
and return will not give up on ourselves, no matter how many times
we have to repeat the process. We will keep telling the truth and
turning around, every day if need be. We will never say never (I'll
never recover, I'll never get it, I'll never learn). Why? Because we
believe in God's goodness more than we believe in our own badness.

> *Those of us who have committed ourselves to a life of*
> *repentance and return will not give up on ourselves, no*
> *matter how many times we have to repeat the process.*

The kind of repentance most of us shrink from is all about us, in
case you hadn't noticed. It is all about me, me, me, the miserable
sinner. No wonder it is so revolting. The other kind of repentance,
the healing kind, is far more interested in God. It spends more time
looking at the kingdom than at the mirror. It has more faith in God's
power to make new than in our own power to mess up.

It is what John the Baptist offered people: a fresh start, a cold
shower, a cure for despair. He offered it as a beginning, not an end.
He knew there was someone coming after him who had something
much stronger to offer, although he did not know who or what that
was. Meanwhile, he was content to be God's watchdog, nipping at
people's heels to get their attention so that they would be wide awake
for what came next.

And no one, I think, was more surprised than he, when he looked up a short time later to see who was wading toward him through the water—not the ax-wielding lumberjack he had expected, not a bigger, meaner guard dog than he, but one as gentle as a child, who gentled even John. Amen.

Chapter Three

Learning to Hate Your Family

| Matthew 10:34-42 | THIS BURR FROM MATTHEW'S GOSPEL is one of those passages I wish he had never written down. I wish a gust of |

wind had scattered all his notes and blown that page away. I wish he had forgotten all about it until he was done with his Gospel and there was no place left to put it. I do not like this passage, because it seems so contrary to what we need in the world right now. The American family is so fragile, so fractured. The last thing we need is another reason to be set against each other, especially a reason decreed by Jesus himself. The last thing we need is a Lord who strides into our living rooms with a sword in his hand to chop us apart. Most of us are already so chopped apart that he would be hard-pressed to put any more distance between us than is already there.

Coming home on an airplane from Chicago, I once sat across from a young boy who was on his way from his mother's home in Illinois to his father's home in Georgia for summer vacation. He was about six and he was traveling alone, which did not seem to bother him nearly as much as it bothered me. I know another couple who divorced when their daughter was three. They were awarded joint custody, which worked well enough when they lived in the same town. Then one of them moved west and their daughter became a frequent flier. Every month, she packs up all her things and heads to the airport, paying the price for her parents' peace. Not too long ago I read about a piece of legislation that would put an end to this sort of thing. In it, the children of a divorce get custody of their home and their parents are granted visitation rights!

None of this is meant to malign divorced parents. In some cases, it was not the divorce that was the mistake but the marriage, and there are children who will freely admit that it is easier to commute between their parents than to live in the crossfire of a household war. Plus, divorce is not the only thing that divides our families. There are parents who abuse their young children, and grown children who abuse their aging parents. There are parents and children who have reached an impasse over money, lifestyle, or religion and no longer speak to each other. There are brothers and sisters who have fought over the same things and have erased each other from their address books. When the separation is mutual it is bad enough, but it is even worse when you have been cut off and you don't know why, or you *do* know why and you want to work it out but you can't, because the telephone number is unlisted and the letters are not answered and the Christmas presents come back marked, "Return to Sender."

This is very painful stuff, about as painful as it gets. Whether it is rejection *by* your family or rejection *of* your family, the rejection itself can consume you, so that you begin to define yourself by it, spending so much time either holding yourself apart from your family or trying to get it back together again that there is precious little time left for anything else. No one knows how to hurt each other the way family members do. The knowledge of one another is so great, the shared history so powerful, the memories so deep—all of them heavy weapons in the arsenals we use against one another. This is no doubt why a large percentage of the homicides in this country take place in homes among family members.

> No one knows how to hurt each other the way family
> members do.

One way we deepen the hurt of a broken family is by tormenting ourselves with the image of a perfect one: a home in which mother and father love each other and stay together forever, in which brothers and sisters are each other's best friends and all the grand-parents are jolly; a home in which everyone sits down at the dinner table together to tell amusing stories and admire one another's accomplishments. With a picture like that floating around in your head, it is hard not to feel like a failure *whatever* your circumstances.

I have two sisters, both of whom live less than two hours away. We see one another a couple of times a year, generally at our parents' house, and we remember one another's birthdays, but that is about it. I used to worry about this, until I started asking around and discovered that very few of my friends are close to their brothers and sisters. We all feel guilty about it, maybe because we were all raised on Louisa May Alcott stories, but the truth is that some families are close and others are not, and close families can have their own set of problems.

> The truth is that some families are close and others are not, and close families can have their own set of problems.

While 50 percent of American families break up, another 50 percent stay together, and a smaller percentage of those stay together quite tightly. Mom and dad rule the roost, kindly but firmly, and children grow up feeling safe and secure. They accept their parents' expectations of them and try to live up to them. The children compete with each other for their parents' affection, and the parents use this competition to shape their children's behavior. It is all done in the name of love, but there can be a lot of control in it, and sometimes it backfires. Children try to leave home and fail. They find they are not equipped to deal with the demands of the adult world and they return home again, where both the rules and the rewards are clear.

One year *New York Times* columnist Anna Quindlen wrote a kind of love letter to her father on Father's Day. In the column, she talked about the simultaneous blessing and curse of being her father's first child. "I was raised as my father's oldest son," she says, detailing his high expectations of her and how she learned to value herself the way her father valued her: for her mind, for her achievements, for her reflection of him. Then one day she stopped, realizing all of a sudden that he and she were two separate people, not mirror images, and much to her surprise she found that she loved him more after that revelation than before. "His expectations were hard on me," she writes now, "but they took me places I would never have gone otherwise. A curse, a blessing, all in one. We might as well have a universal support group: Adult Children of Parents."

You think I have forgotten about the gospel, but I have not. I think Jesus knew how powerful families are in our lives, whether they are working too well or not at all, whether we are snuggled down deep in the bosom of them or utterly estranged from them. I think he knew how easy it is for us to be consumed by them so that we forget who we are apart from them—and I also think he knew that it is only when we discover who we are apart from them that we can be part of them in a healthy way.

I am a daughter, a wife, a sister, an aunt, and each of those identities has shaped my life, but none of them contains me. I am Barbara. I am Christian. I am a child of God. That is my true identity, and all the others grow out of it. Each of you has your own list of roles. Most of you are children *and* parents, but like me, you are God's child first. That is no role. That is who you most truly are. That is where your true peace and security lie. When you know that—when you have learned the truth of it in your heart as well as your head—then chances are that you will survive a broken family and go on to choose a better one from the people whom God sends your way. And when you know that, chances are that you will not be swallowed up by an intact family whose love has a little too much control in it. In both cases, knowing your true identity can make all the difference. It can help save your life.

We do not have to hate our families in order to remember who we are apart from them. The truth about Matthew's community is that many of them were already estranged from their families. In his time, it was the custom for whole households to adopt the faith of their heads. Everyone in the house was compelled to believe what that person believed—spouses, children, servants, everyone—so if one of them elected to become a Christian it was nothing short of mutiny, especially since becoming a Christian had all kinds of consequences.

> *We do not have to hate our families in order to remember who we are apart from them.*

It might mean selling all that a person owned and giving it to the poor. It might mean beginning to associate with a whole new class of people that included outlaws and slaves. It would certainly mean bringing the whole household under suspicion of the Roman Empire, so there were plenty of people sitting in Matthew's congregation who had already been kicked out of their families for believing in Jesus. When Matthew told them what Jesus said about hating their families, it did not frighten them. It comforted them. It was as though he had known what would happen to them and had reassured them ahead of time.

We live in a different world with different consequences for believing in God, but one thing that has not changed is our deep desire for kinship. Some of us find that in our families and some of us do not. Some of us find it in our church families and some of us do not. Whether we do or don't, however, Jesus' demand remains the same. We are to love him above all other loves, and if that means losing those we love, we are not to fear, because buried in the demand is a promise: that what we lose for his sake we shall find again, returned to us more alive than ever before. Amen.

Chapter Four

Divine Anger

Ephesians 4:25–5:2

EVEN BEFORE IT BECAME POLITICIZED, one of the most popular books of the nineties was *The Book of Virtues*, edited by William J. Bennett. Subtitled *A Treasury of Great Moral Stories*, it is full of poems, hymns, fables, and true stories that Bennett has organized under headings such as "Compassion," "Responsibility," "Honesty," "Self-Discipline," and "Faith." He wrote it, he said, as a how-to book for moral literacy, a kind of primer on the do's and don'ts of life with others. He also wrote it as a source of encouragement. "There is a lot we read of or experience in life that is not so encouraging," he says in his introduction. "This book, I hope, does otherwise. . . . I hope it points us to 'the better angels of our nature.' "[1]

Paul could have said the same thing about his Letter to the Ephesians. Written from his jail cell while the known world fell apart, his letter is a treasury of his own teachings, meant to encourage the faithful in a way of life that was in danger of extinction. "Let all of us speak the truth to our neighbors, for we are members of one another," he coached them. "Be angry but do not sin." "Be kind to one another, tenderhearted, forgiving one another, as God in Christ has forgiven you."

If the Christian church has lost its moral authority in our time, it is at least partly because we have not taken Paul's advice. We have our own book of virtues, but we still struggle with its teaching. We do not, on the whole, speak the truth to our neighbors. We are polite but noncommittal, wanting above all to be liked. We do not live as though we were members of one another. We fight with as much malevolence as any bunch of pagans, dividing ourselves into "us" and "them" at the drop of a hat. We are not kind so much as we are nice, which is about as bland a virtue as you can find, if it is a virtue at all. Like the little girl with the curl in the middle of her forehead, when we are good we are almost too good and when we are bad we are horrid.

Paul has a different vision of Christian community. Niceness does not concern him. He does not give two hoots about being liked. No one ever taught him that if you cannot say something nice you should not say anything at all. He knows that when real people live in real community with one another, they will discover real differences and suffer real discord. This is true whether the community is a marriage, a family, a neighborhood, a church, or a whole society. It is not possible to love one another without also hating one another from time to time. When that time comes, Paul says, do not shut up and disappear. Speak the truth in love. Be angry but do not sin. "Be kind to one another, tenderhearted, forgiving one another, as God in Christ has forgiven you."

Very few of us were ever taught that anger is part of true love. Even fewer of us have been taught how to handle our anger so that it is part of our health and not part of our sickness. Paul seems to know that being angry and sinning are two different things. The one does not have to lead to the other. It often does, which is why so many of us were taught to hide our anger, but it is entirely possible to be angry with people without sinning—that is, without separating ourselves from them or hurting them in order to spare ourselves the same thing.

> Very few of us were ever taught that anger is part of true love.

At its most basic level, anger is what is called an "emergency emotion." Someone or something threatens you—your safety, your loved ones, your home, your values, your self-esteem—and some very predictable things happen inside of you. Your heart rate and blood pressure go up. Your pupils dilate. Your breathing gets shallow and your blood flows away from your hands and feet (in case of injury), which gives you sweaty palms. Your body is now physically prepared to fight the threat or to flee it, but none of this is a conscious decision on your part. It is a reflex, that is all—your body's ancient way of defending itself against danger. Meanwhile, all your mind knows is that you are M-A-D. Right underneath that madness, of course, is mortal fear, but the mind translates this into anger for purposes of self-defense. This fits well with human nature, which seems to prefer "I'm mad" to "I'm afraid."

So there you have it. A hoodlum jumps into your path. Your bloodstream fills with adrenaline and either you give the guy a karate chop or you run for your life, fueled with energy that seems to have come out of nowhere. This is what we call anger—a strong feeling of displeasure at a perceived threat, accompanied by a rush of energy we can use to flee or fight back. I call it one of God's good gifts—our ability to recognize danger and respond to it—only like so many of God's gifts, it has some real subtleties to it.

There are all kinds of ways we can mishandle our anger so that it hurts us instead of helping us. The most popular way is to deny it, especially when the threat is a minor one such as a friend who is always ten minutes later than she says she will be. "Oh, gosh, I've done it again," she says, looking at your watch (she doesn't wear one). "Are you mad at me?"

"Nonsense," you say, smiling at her through clenched teeth. "I'm just glad you're here." You *are* mad, but it seems petty of you to say so, so what you do instead is you save it up and you save it up until one day your friend arrives at her usual time and you take her apart limb by limb. "What is the matter with you? Do you ever think of anyone but yourself? My time is as valuable as yours is, in case you didn't know, and I am sick and tired of twiddling my thumbs while you take your sweet time doing whatever it is you do while I sit here waiting for you!"

Almost no one denies anger successfully. It either erupts like that or else it burrows inward. You blame yourself for getting mad in the first place. You tell yourself that you are a wretched person, that you should be able to forgive those who trespass against you no matter what they have done to you, and you resolve once again to ignore your anger in hopes that it will go away. Only it does not go away. It just turns into an ulcer or a bad back or a depression that deepens every day.

Almost no one denies anger successfully.

Some people seek help at this point, and the advice they often get is to "let their anger out." If that is as far as they go, they generally become walking volcanoes, spewing unpleasantness on whoever gets in their way. It is a surprising thing, but psychological studies show that venting anger does not diminish angry feelings. It actually increases them, by stimulating that emergency emotion all over again.

So what is an angry person to do? "Be angry but do not sin," Paul says. Speak the truth. Be kind. Forgive one another, as God in Christ has forgiven you. There is another way, which begins with Paul's distinction between the emotion of anger and the sin of anger. The emotion is nothing more than a flashing red light that says, "Danger here." Granted, it tends to come with a surge of energy that can make you dizzy, but it is up to us what we will do with that surge. The crucial thing, for me, is to take responsibility for my anger. It is mine, and it is subject to my interpretation. The more curious I can become about it, the better.

Why am I feeling threatened? Is the threat real? Is it intentional? What is my own part in what is going on? Have I got my facts straight? If Paul is right that we are members of one another, then my enemy is part of me. What part, I wonder? Is there something I hate in him because it is easier than hating it in myself? Most important of all, where is God in all this? What is my anger trying to teach me?

Your mother taught you to count to ten when you were mad so that you could think about these things. If we would still count to ten—or ten hundred, maybe—chances are that we might have something decent to say when we opened our mouths again. We might be able to say how we feel and what we want from our neighbors without expecting them to change on the spot because we said so. We might learn to express ourselves so that we can be heard—without blame or bitterness—and to listen as carefully as we wish to be listened to ourselves. We might even figure out how to be imitators of God.

Christians, of all people, should know that there is such a thing as a good fight. Read the Bible! God fought with those God loved the most: Abraham, Moses, David, Job. Jacob wrestled the angel. Jonah got sent to his room inside a great fish. Jesus yelled at his disciples as if they were a bunch of truant schoolboys. He called the Pharisees every name he could think of in order to get their attention, but from day one, divine anger has been anger that means to heal and not to harm, to unite and not to divide. That is what makes a fight a good one, and every one of us can learn how.

> *Christians, of all people, should know that there is such a thing as a good fight.*

Contrary to popular opinion, Christians are not nice, polite people who never get angry with one another. Those are not our virtues. Our virtues are truth-telling, kindness, forgiveness, and yes, even anger—as long as it is the anger that is part of true love—through which we move closer to one another and to the God who has shown us how it is done. Amen.

Chapter Five

Feeding the Enemy

Romans 12:9-21

IN THE TWELFTH CHAPTER OF HIS Letter to the Romans, Paul preaches his own version of the sermon on the mount. In twelve short verses he turns out thirty instructions, all of them meant to put flesh on the bones of Christ's one commandment of love. Paul had good reason for going to so much trouble. The church in Rome was splitting apart in at least two different ways. Inside, by conflict between Jewish and Gentile Christians. And outside, by conflict between Christian and non-Christian Romans. There were black eyes and bad feelings all over the place. Marcus went to the midweek service so he would not have to sit in the same room with Clovis on Sunday, Lucius was so mad at both of them that he had quit coming to church at all, and Chloe had just bought herself a pit bull to keep her pagan neighbors from cutting through her yard.

It was a mess, all the way around. People said they believed that God was love. They said they believed in the power of goodness, at least until someone crossed them. Then goodness and love fell pretty much by the wayside and retaliation turned out to be what they believed in after all. If you have ever been on the receiving end of a really grievous wrong, then you know how your mind works.

This is wrong, you tell yourself. *I am in a lot of pain here. This should not have happened to me. Someone should pay for this. Evildoers must be stopped, and if I don't do it someone else will get hurt. It's not my nature, but I will strike back. I will fight fire with fire. God is a God of justice, after all, and what has happened to me is not right, not by any reckoning.*

That is how it usually works. Then the lawsuit is filed, the insult is returned, the line is drawn, and the cold war begins, full of stony silence and clenched teeth. Because something deep down inside of us believes that we will be annihilated if we do not fight back.

> *Something deep down inside of us believes that we will be annihilated if we do not fight back.*

I still remember my nephew Will's first birthday party. He was as round and bald as a Buddha at that point, still hovering on the verge of speech. Never out of his parents' sight, he was a typical only child—used to being the center of attention—only he was not spoiled yet, because he had not yet learned how to manipulate love for his own ends. He just thought everyone was loved the way he was, and he gave it away as fast as he got it.

There were only a handful of us there that day—Will's parents, aunts, and grandparents, plus his godparents and their seven-year-old son, Jason. After the cake and the singing and the presents were all over, Will let us know how pleased he was by doing his new dance for us—a shy twirling in place that he had invented several days before with lots of fancy arm work.

We were all circled around him admiring his dance when Jason simply could not stand it anymore. He charged through the circle, put both of his hands on Will's chest, and shoved. Will fell hard. His rear end hit first, then his head, with a crack. He looked utterly surprised at first. No one had ever hurt him before, and he did not know what to make of it. Then he opened up his mouth and howled, but not for long. His mother hugged him and helped him to his feet and the first thing Will did was to totter over to Jason. He knew Jason was at the bottom of this thing, only since no one had ever been mean to him before he did not know what the thing was. So he did what he had always done. He put his arms around Jason and lay his head against that mean little boy's body, and at that moment all my Christian conviction went right out the door.

I will buy him a BB gun for his next birthday, I thought. *Iron knuckles. A karate video for toddlers.* It just about killed me, to think how that sweet child would have to learn to defend himself, but it was either that or eat dust on the playground the rest of his life, with some bully's foot on the back of his head.

Only according to Paul, Will was right and I was wrong. "Do not repay anyone evil for evil," he wrote the Romans, "but take thought for what is noble in the sight of all." What Will did to Jason put an end to the meanness in that room. What I wanted to do to Jason would only have multiplied it. Paul's advice is idealistic, impractical, and dangerous to one's health, but there it is: "Do not be overcome by evil, but overcome evil with good."

All I can figure is that Paul had incredible faith in the power of love, faith that most of us either do not share or are not eager to test. He seemed to understand that the real enemy is not whoever pushes us down in the middle of our dance but whatever it is inside of us that wants to leap up and push back. Evil is never satisfied with controlling one side of a situation. Its goal is to infect everyone involved—the victim along with the bully, the plaintiff along with the defendant, the offended along with the offender. When everyone has his or her dukes in the air and there is a loaded gun in every household (did you know that is a city ordinance in Kennesaw, Georgia?), then the enemy will have won, because the whole point is to recruit the good guys by making them believe they are stopping the bad guys.

The real enemy is not whoever pushes us down in the middle of our dance but whatever it is inside of us that wants to leap up and push back.

That is not how to do it! Paul says, "Bless those who persecute you; bless and do not curse them." Because the moment you curse them, you join them, and however good it may feel at the moment, it is still a surrender. The only way to conquer evil is to absorb it, Paul says. Take it into yourself and disarm it. Neutralize its acids. Serve as a charcoal filter for its smog. Suck it up, put a straitjacket on it and turn it over to God, so that when you breathe out again the air is pure.

It is an incredible dare, and Paul apparently knows very few of us will accept it unless there is something in it for us, so he adds a little bonus near the end. "If your enemies are hungry, feed them; if they are thirsty, give them something to drink; for by doing this you will heap burning coals on their heads." Nice talk, Paul! Convince us to care for our enemies by telling us how much it will hurt them if we do!

I don't know what that crazy sentence is all about. Martin Luther thought it meant that those who are converted by love "burn against themselves," once they have discovered what they have been missing. All I know is that the first half of the sentence renders the second half harmless. People who come upon their enemies in a weakened state and who resist the temptation to take advantage of them—who help them instead, giving those who have hurt them food and drink—those people are already out of danger. By the time they have packed the picnic basket and filled the thermos with pink lemonade, I guarantee you they will have forgotten about the burning coal part. "Do I not conquer my enemy," said Abraham Lincoln, "by making him my friend?"

There is nothing sentimental or the least bit easy about any of this. There is not even a guarantee that it will work, but one thing is for sure: When we repay evil with evil, evil is all there is, in bigger and more toxic piles. The only way to reverse the process is to behave in totally unexpected ways—blessing the persecutor, feeding the enemy, embracing the bully—breaking the vicious cycle by refusing to participate in it anymore.

> *When we repay evil with evil, evil is all there is, in bigger and more toxic piles.*

That is what love is, Paul says: not a warm feeling between like-minded friends but plain old imitation of Christ, who took all the meanness of the world and ran it through the filter of his own body, repaying evil with good, blame with pardon, death with life. Call it divine reverse psychology. It worked once and it can work again, whenever God can find someone else willing to give it a try. Amen.

Chapter Six

The Betrayer in Our Midst

John 13:21-35 | JUDAS'S BETRAYAL MAY BE THE MOST famous one in all of history, not only because of whom he betrays but also because of who he is—not an enemy outsider but one of the inner circle who has been with Jesus from the start. What could be more treacherous than that?

Because we know how things turn out in the end we tend to imagine him as a fringe member of the group—the suspicious looking redhead who is always standing off to one side all by himself—but it is not true. If anything, he is the most trusted of the twelve friends, the one whom they put in charge of the money box. It is his job to keep food on the table, for them and for the poor. He is their stewardship chairman. They trust him to manage their resources and to share them wisely, because Judas is one of them. He is the Lord's friend. He has walked hundreds of miles with them and sat talking around the cookfire with them and slept out under the stars with them.

Judas was there at the wedding in Cana when Jesus turned water into wine and he was there when five thousand people stuffed themselves on five loaves and two fish. He saw the lame man pick up his pallet and walk and he watched the blind man's eyes focus for the first time. He was there when Jesus shouted Lazarus from his tomb and he has just had his feet washed by the one who did all this. If

Judas had really been the odd man out, the others would have known right away whom Jesus was talking about at dinner that night, but they did not.

"Very truly, I tell you, one of you will betray me," he said, and they all stopped chewing to look at one another, because they could not imagine who it might be.

This betrayal by an intimate is the stuff nightmares are made of. Witness the frightening appeal of movies like *Deceived* and *The Hand that Rocks the Cradle* or best-sellers like *The Firm*. You think you know someone well and find out that you do not. Your successful business keeps losing money and when you run an audit you learn that your trusted partner has robbed you blind. Or you come home one afternoon to find your young daughter in tears and she tells you that her uncle—your brother—has been coming into her bedroom at night. Or you are opening the mail one afternoon when you discover that your spouse—who has been acting strange lately—has taken out a large insurance policy on your life.

> *This betrayal by an intimate is the stuff nightmares are made of.*

Betrayal can be as dramatic as that, or much simpler. A friend gossips about you behind your back. A co-worker uses privileged information to steal your best account. A parent disapproves of the person you love and fires you from the family. Betrayal by strangers is hard enough, but betrayal by those closest to you is a killer. It destroys trust, it robs the past, it deadens the heart. In Dante's *Inferno*, the lowest circle of hell is reserved for such traitors. There Judas, Brutus, and Cassius are frozen in ice for all eternity, but even Dante is clear that it is Judas Iscariot who will suffer the most, for he betrayed his friend with a kiss.

It is entirely possible that this betrayal is the deepest pain Jesus will undergo in the days to come. First Judas, then the rest of the inner circle, then the treachery of the crowd—his own people—choosing to free the bandit Barabbas instead of their long-awaited king. Physical pain is one thing, but this is another. To be abandoned by those who are closest to him, to be stabbed from behind by those who know him best—this is as wounding as the fat nails that finally pin him to the cross.

The terrible wisdom hidden in this story is that the church has far less to fear from outsiders than from insiders. We are much more likely to encounter the enemy within our midst than in the world beyond our doors. It reminds me of something I once saw written on the ceiling of a summer camp dining hall: "We are the people our parents told us to watch out for." To understand Judas is to understand the shadow side of the church where we—yes we—have it in us to betray those we love.

> *The terrible wisdom hidden in this story is that the church has far less to fear from outsiders than from insiders.*

But it is not possible to understand Judas without understanding Jesus as well, because Judas does not act in a vacuum. His choice is a chilling one, but it is not the only one in the story. Jesus makes choices too, choices that may change the way we see the one Judas makes.

I don't know anyone who doesn't wonder about Judas's role in the drama. Was he a true villain or just a divine pawn? If scripture was going to be fulfilled, then *someone* had to betray Jesus. "Do quickly what you have to do." That is how it reads in the New English Bible—as an assignment, not a choice. Was Judas really the bad guy, or was he just the unlucky one who drew the short straw?

And if he was the bad guy, then why? Was it just plain greed for what blood money could buy, or was it deep disappointment that Jesus had not turned out to be the kind of Messiah Judas had hoped he would be? According to legend, Judas was the zealot among Jesus' disciples—the one who was ready to fight the Romans to the death and who longed for a Messiah who would lead the battle. He was the one who had a real crown in mind for Jesus, not a circlet of thorns. When it became clear that Jesus was not going to meet his expectations, it was Judas who believed *he* had been betrayed. And if that is what led him to do what he did, then God knows he was not the first or last human being who turned murderous when someone he loved failed to make his dreams come true.

Whatever Judas's degree of guilt and whatever his motive, it is extremely important to note that Jesus identifies his betrayer by feeding him. Not by turning over the table and casting him out. Not by tying him to his chair so he cannot carry out his plan, but by feeding him—dipping a morsel into his own cup and giving it to Judas, whose feet he has just washed, bathing them with warm water and drying them with the towel he wears around his waist.

Knowing who Judas is and what he is about to do, Jesus does not throw him out. He bathes him and feeds him, which means that Judas is never—never—excluded from the circle of friends. He is included until he excludes himself, and when he goes out, John tells us, it is *night*—inside of him and outside of him, as dark as dark can be.

But as soon as he is gone, Jesus begins speaking not of darkness but of light. "Now the Son of Man has been glorified," he says, "and God has been glorified in him. If God has been glorified in him, God will also glorify him in himself and will glorify him at once." What a lot of glory! Has Judas turned the light off or turned it on? By doing quickly what he has to do, he has set everything in motion. Soon the soldiers will come and the crowd will cry for blood and the sentence will be pronounced: "Crucify him!" Soon Jesus will be scourged and crowned and lifted high on the cross. It will not look like glory to anyone but God, but Jesus knows. He knows that his death will shine like the sun, and that the time has come for him to practice what he has been preaching.

It is time to lay down his life for his friends, but before he does, he gives them a new commandment—that they love one another as he is about to love them. That is how people will know who they are, because they love one another like that. It is his last will and testament, and their community charter as well. Everything else he has taught them is important, but this is crucial: Their love for one another will be the one true mark of their discipleship. Not their knowledge, nor their piety, nor their good works, but that death-defying love that is his glory and shall be theirs as well.

And Judas? What about Judas? He has excluded himself from this fellowship and from this final teaching—a message that might have saved his life had he stayed to hear it—but he has not stayed. He has disappeared into the night, kicking the rock that will bring the avalanche down upon them. He has removed himself beyond their reach—Judas, the sinner, the devil in disciples' clothing, the traitor frozen in the lowest circle of hell, who deserves everything he gets and more—but here is what I want to know.

Does Jesus die for him too? When he lays down his life for his friends, does that include Judas? "The one who ate my bread has lifted his heel against me," Jesus said just moments before we tuned in (13:18). He was quoting Psalm 41:9, which tells us that he knew, all along—knew that one of those sitting around his table would turn on him—and if he had been anyone else, he would have started watching what he said around them, holding himself back until he could ferret out the traitor and expel him, or worse.

But he was not someone else. He was the Messiah, who washed his friends' feet—knowing full well one of them would betray him— and who fed them their supper—knowing full well one of them would betray him. He was the Lord, who went on giving himself away to the one who would give him away, because his faithfulness did not depend on theirs. When he dipped the morsel in his cup and handed

> *He was the Lord, who went on giving himself away to the one who would give him away, because his faithfulness did not depend on theirs.*

it to Judas, he not only revealed who Judas was, he also revealed who he was. The one who feeds his enemies—who goes on treating them as friends—loving them to the end.

What that means, I think, is that Judas is indispensable to our understanding of holy communion. Judas, of all people! His presence at the last supper is our lasting reminder that this is a meal not only for the good, the right, the faithful among us, but also for the crooks and double-crossers, the spies and impostors. It will reveal us for who we are—make no mistake about that—and that knowledge may send us running from the room into the dark, dark night.

But it may also allow us to stay put, clinging to the edge of the table for dear life if need be, or better yet, clinging to the presence of the Lord at the head of the table, whose faithfulness does not depend on ours and whose death-defying love knows no end. He is the food and drink that saves our lives, thawing our frozen hearts by taking them into his own. He is the broken, poured-out one who gives himself to us, offering to feed us again and again. Amen.

Chapter Seven

Buried by Baptism

Romans 6:3-5

ONE OF THE THINGS I LIKE BEST ABOUT the church is the processions, especially on grand occasions like baptisms and ordinations. You watch people come into the church one way and you know they will go out another way. The procession is like a parade to a royal wedding, or a coronation.

I do not know what ordinations are like in your church, but in my denomination they sometimes have this flavor about them. I remember one ordination I went to back in the seventies, at Christ Church, New Haven. The procession began with a very agile thurifer, who filled the nave with sweet smoke by twirling the incense pot in figure eights over his head. Then came a sea of clergy and choir, separated into their respective orders by three different sets of crucifers and acolytes. Finally the ordinand appeared, vested in white. He was surrounded by his sponsors, and behind them came the bishop in full dress, clumping his crozier on the ground as he walked.

The next two hours were something of a blur, but I do remember the moment the ordinand lay face down on the floor at the foot of the steps to the altar. His body made a perfect cross. I wondered how the cold stones felt on his cheek. Then he got up and was helped into a gold brocade vestment that twinkled like a thousand candles, in which he went to serve the altar as a deacon for the first time.

It was memorable, obviously, and I imagine I was not the only person there who thought becoming a deacon must be the next best thing to ascending a throne, but what you and I both know is that come Monday, or Tuesday at the latest, someone at the church was telling that young man that the lightbulb in the women's restroom had burned out and could he please do something about it before the following Sunday?

I don't want to sound cynical, because I love what I do, only it is not what I expected. I thought I would spend hours in a leather chair, reading books, writing sermons, and keeping appointments with those who sought my counsel. I thought I would remember people's birthdays and answer letters on time. I thought I would pray more. Instead, I return telephone calls, pay bills, break up fights, cause them. I proofread bulletins, take the church cat to the vet, and make sure everyone has read the sexual misconduct policy manual so we qualify for our insurance.

> I don't want to sound cynical, because I love what I do, only it is not what I expected.

I also complain, as I am doing right now. It seems to go with the territory, and all in all I do not know anyone who can complain better than a bunch of ordained ministers. Maybe it is because the work really is hard, but I think it is more than that. I think it is because we were expecting something different, something—well—*holier* than this.

And yet I have noticed that there is a certain boastfulness to our complaining. We sound like people who have stayed up all night with a colicky baby and want everyone to know how exhausting, how exasperating, how absolutely consuming it is to have a child who needs you like that, who depends on you all the time for everything— and whom you would not give up for anything, incidentally, whose very need is part of your bond, because it is wonderful to be necessary like that, to serve someone who so clearly requires what you have to offer.

If you interviewed any of those parents, they would probably tell you that staying up all night was not what they had in mind when they decided to have a baby. They were thinking of Little League, ballet, bedtime stories, Christmas. They were thinking of someone who looked like them, whose breath smelled of pink gum when she pressed her face against theirs and said, "Momma, Poppa, I love you."

It was mostly romance, in other words: 5 percent fact, 15 percent hearsay, and 80 percent fantasy. And yet for something so ephemeral, romance is an incredibly potent motivator. Without romance, we might never bind ourselves to one other person and learn how to negotiate a life together. Without romance, we might never decide to bear children and find out what it means to give our life for the life of another. It is a kind of trick in which the object of our desire is swapped in midair. We reach for our illusions. What we lay hold of is the truth. It can be shocking, sometimes, but it is also salvific, because without the ideal, we might never grasp the reality. So I have this budding theory that romance is how life gets us where life needs us to be. And by extension, that the romance of ordination is how God tricks us into servanthood.

We think we are volunteering for a life of holy order, which of course turns out to be nothing but washing feet—a whole parade of them, in every shape and size, along with wet towels, muddy water, and a chronic shortage of soap. It is exactly what God told us it would be—no more, no less—but somehow we forgot. We were thinking of leather chairs, pulpits, prayer desks, Christmas. Without the romance, we might never have volunteered, but thank God for the romance. It is how we get where life needs us to be.

Jesus' own ordination happened at his baptism. He had every right to stay dry that day. He had nothing on his conscience the way everyone else did who lined up at river's edge, but for reasons unknown to us he got in line too and took his turn under the water. When he came up, God laid hands on him in the form of a dove. "This is my Son, the Beloved, with whom I am well pleased."

> *We think we are volunteering for a life of holy order, which of course turns out to be nothing but washing feet.*

It was a much bigger deal than what I saw in New Haven. Jesus might well have expected a stellar ministry after something like that, but the very next thing that happened was that the spirit led him into the wilderness to be teased by all the power he would never have: no magic, no special protection, no control over the kingdoms of this world. Just a life of serving God, in any form that service might take.

I don't know if you ever thought about it this way before, but ordination, like baptism, is the celebration of a demotion. Unlike sorority initiations or Eagle Scout ceremonies, it is a rite in which we step down, not up. It is a ritual in which we are made the servants of all, and it seems to me that there is rich irony in our lining up to do this kind of work. Would any of us answer a classified ad that said, "Menial labor, long hours, high expectations, low pay"? And yet here we are. Willingly. Some of us having gone into considerable debt for the privilege.

Now I am thinking of another service I attended at Christ Church (isn't it interesting what you can learn from liturgy?), this one a baptism at the Easter Vigil. The candidate was a three-year-old girl named Ellen whose parents wanted her baptized by immersion, which was problematic in a church with a traditional birdbath baptismal font. No one had asked Ellen about it, but the priest in charge accepted the challenge and finally came up with a thirty-six-gallon garbage can that he decorated with ivy.

It was very pretty if you did not look at it too hard, but it fooled no one, least of all Ellen. When she came into the dark church that night and saw it sitting there at the back of the center aisle, she stiffened. But she was a brave little girl whose parents had rehearsed her well, so she did everything she was supposed to do right up until the priest leaned down to pick her up.

"Don't do it!" she screamed then, planting her feet flat against the garbage can so that water slopped everywhere. "Don't do it!" I cannot for the life of me remember what happened after that, but I will never forget the sound of that child's voice banging through the high rafters of the church.

All right, she was only three years old, but her instincts were good. She knew she was about to be killed, and she wanted no part of it. If you prefer a more mature witness, take Ambrose of Milan, who had the same reaction. He was governor of Upper Italy in the mid–fourth century—a nominal Christian who had never been baptized (don't ask me why). Maybe because preparation for baptism could take years in those days. Maybe because he did not want his life to change that much, but at any rate, there he was minding his own business in the governor's office one day when he was called to Milan to keep the peace.

The church there was determined to elect a bishop, although the Arian and Orthodox parties were equally determined to put each other out of business. Ambrose waded right into the middle of their quarrel and so impressed everyone with his gifts that they elected him bishop on the spot. The way I heard the story, he ran for his life, but the crowd hunted him down, baptized him, and stuffed a mitre on his head, all in one day.

"Do you not know that all of us who have been baptized into Christ Jesus were baptized into his death?" That is how Paul put it, and the answer is yes, we know. We just forget sometimes, but—thanks be to God—life keeps on reminding us. Every day that we get up, review our carefully planned agendas, and watch the whole thing go to hell by 10:00 A.M., we remember. Every day that we set out to be God's gifts to humankind and end up shouting at the church treasurer, we remember. Every day that we mean to change the world and end up washing one person's feet, we remember. "Therefore we have been buried with him by baptism into death"—Why?—"so that, just as Christ was raised from the dead by the glory of the Father, so we too might walk in newness of life."

Our illusions may bring us to the service of God, but it is only after they have died that we become the servants of God, delivered from our own ideas about who we are and what we are supposed to be doing to God's own idea, which generally passes all understanding. One thing we can count on, I believe, is that God's idea will have no illusion in it. It will be as real as any of the people who present themselves to us each day, asking us for attention, for love, for conflict, for any proof that they matter, to us or to God.

> *Our illusions may bring us to the service of God, but it is only after they have died that we become the servants of God.*

They are not very romantic figures, most of them, but they are Jesus in disguise, and so are we. He told us so. When we learn to serve them the way they are instead of the way we wish they would be, real life begins. They even begin to serve us too, by reminding us of all the power we will never have: no magic, no special protection, no control over the kingdoms of the world. Just a life of serving God, in any form that service might take.

I also believe God's idea is about newness of life, just as Paul said. That is why we are buried by baptism—so that we may rise to new life—not the one we had planned, perhaps, nor the one we expected, but the one it has pleased God to give us. May your own ministries be full of that life. May you rejoice in the loss of your illusions and celebrate the prospect of your demotion, and may all your complaints be laced with joy. Amen.

The Suffering Cup

Matthew 20:17-28

HERE IS ONE OF THOSE EMBARRASSing little stories that make you glad you were not around when Matthew was collecting material for his book. Poor James and John. They wanted to go down in history and they did, as two grown men who got their mother to ask their boss for special treatment. One reason it is so embarrassing, I think, is because it could have been any of us, trying to squeeze a favor from Jesus. James and John just happened to get caught.

> *Poor James and John. They wanted to go down in history and they did, as two grown men who got their mother to ask their boss for special treatment.*

If you have ever been friends with someone who became famous, then you can sympathize. It is such a kick to be close to someone who generates all that electricity. Maybe it is because we hope some of their fame will rub off on us or maybe it is just satisfying to know someone who has achieved a semblance of the Good Life. While you are watching your college roommate being interviewed for television, you can turn to someone and say, "I remember when he wore his hair in a ponytail and had a moustache down to here. . . ." But the whole time, what you are really hoping is that he will look into your part of the crowd, shield his eyes from the lights, and say, "I can't believe it! Is it really you? Quiet, everyone! I want you to meet my best old friend, who has materialized out of the blue tonight." Then he will pull you into the circle of light, invite you to join him for dinner, and bump someone else down a place so that you can sit right next to him. That is as good as it gets—recognition, affection, rank—and all because you knew him when.

That is what the Zebedee brothers want, or rather, it is what their mother wants, although the fact that she addresses Jesus and Jesus addresses her sons is a clue that he knows they have put her up to it. What they want is to sit right next to Jesus when he becomes king of the kingdom—one on his right hand and one on his left. They do not care what their titles turn out to be—chancellor and provost would be fine, or first and second vice presidents. They just want to make sure that they have reserved seat stubs in their pockets when the time comes, and apparently they think it will sound better coming from their mother than from them.

It is not an unreasonable request, on the face of it. They are two of his first disciples, after all. Simon Peter and his brother Andrew were the very first, but James and his brother John were next—disciples numbers three and four—and for some time it was just the four of them, following Jesus around as he began his ministry in Galilee. Even after Jesus had recruited all twelve of the disciples, Peter, James, and John remained his special friends. According to Matthew, they were the only ones he took with him to witness his transfiguration. They were the only ones he begged to stay awake with him in the garden of Gethsemane. While they understand him no better than the others, he clearly considers them his confidants and shows a marked preference for their company. Why shouldn't they assume that he will continue to prefer them once he has come into his kingdom?

Of course, that is where their lack of understanding comes in. The brothers' request might have made sense at some other time or place, but here it comes right on the heels of Jesus' description of what "coming into his own" will mean. He has just told them that he is about to be condemned to death. He has just told them that he is about to be mocked, flogged, and crucified. It is the third time he has told them, in fact, and every time it is as if they do not hear him. The first time he told them, Peter objected. "God forbid it, Lord! This must never happen to you!" The second time he told them, they argued among themselves about who was the greatest.

Now he tells them for the third time, which is when the Zebedee brothers get their mother to ask him for two good seats in the kingdom. It is enough to make you wonder what is going on here. Do they have any sense of what he is trying to tell them? And if they do, then why do they keep changing the subject?

In the first place, no doubt, because what he is telling them scares them to death. He is the most promising character they have ever known. They have invested everything in his success, and here he is telling them to get ready for his funeral. It is not something they want to hear, so they do what any of us might do—they tell him to stop it and lighten up. They talk about something else. They block out what he is saying about himself because it interferes with what they are saying about themselves, such as who is the greatest, such as who will sit where when the good times roll.

And it is only partly due to their self-absorption. The rest of it is due to their genuine confidence in Jesus—that he is a winner, that they are playing on a championship team, and that wherever he is going, no matter how he gets there, they are going with him. The details do not faze them one bit. They believe he can handle anything, and once he has, they plan to be right there beside him—his chiefs of staff, his board of trustees.

It is easy to judge James and John, especially from this distance, but they are only doing what all of us do in one way or another. They have a vision of the Good Life and they know someone who can help them get there, someone they will do anything for if only he will remember them when he comes into his own. They will knock on doors, serve soup, sleep on a different pull-out bed every night if they have to. They will follow him anywhere as long as there is an end in sight—a time when he will be declared the winner and they can all go to the victory party, where they will find their names stenciled in gold leaf on chairs at the head table.

That is what the Zebedee brothers want, and when the other disciples hear about it they are angry, Matthew tells us, but Jesus is not. If anything he sounds sad—sad that he cannot give them what they want, sad that what they want is not his to give. "You do not know what you are asking," he tells them, but when they assure him that they do know, that they are able to drink his cup, you can almost see his face crumple.

"You will indeed drink my cup," he says to them, "but to sit at my right hand and at my left, this is not mine to grant." They have, in other words, asked the right person for the wrong thing. They have asked the shepherd for individual retirement accounts. They have asked the footwasher for alligator shoes. They have asked the carpenter's son for box seats in paradise, and none of them is his to give. He can heal lepers and cast out demons; he can give sight to the blind and he can even raise the dead, but he cannot confer status or guarantee income or grant heavenly perks, because he does not have any of them to give.

> *They have, in other words, asked the right person for the wrong thing.*

He is a servant through and through—not someone temporarily disguised as a servant who will soon throw off his rags and call a press conference, but someone who will keep on disappearing into the crowd of hungry people who follow him around. He loves nothing better than touching them, feeding them, talking with them, only this is no campaign strategy for him. This is his way of life—truly, the Good Life for him—but not the one James and John had in mind, which is why he cannot give it to them. All he can give them is his own life. It is a life lived with and for others, although often without reward; a life of meaning and purpose, although often obscured; a life of long days and short nights on the move with no travel allowance, no first-class accommodations or executive privileges—in short, a life of sacrifice but a life worth living beyond a shadow of a doubt, a life with so much life in it that death cannot touch it, not even with a cross.

"Are you able to drink the cup that I am about to drink?" he asks the brothers who want to sit next to him. "We are able," they answer, straightening their shoulders before they step into the circle of light and face the cameras with their friend. What they do not know is that he is headed in the opposite direction. He is about to yank out all the plugs and lead them into the darkest place they have ever been.

They do not have a clue what they are saying, in other words, no more than any of us knows what we are saying when we ask Jesus to keep us close to him. He may not be able to fulfill our fantasies about

> *They do not have a clue what they are saying, in other words,
> no more than any of us knows what we are saying when we
> ask Jesus to keep us close to him.*

what that means, but I believe he will answer our prayer all the same—by giving us a life as much like his as we can stand—and maybe even by giving us the grace to discover that it is the Good Life after all. Amen.

Chapter Nine

Pick Up Your Cross

Matthew 16:21-27

A FRIEND OF MINE TELLS A STORY about her eldest son, Jeff, who adored his grandfather above all other mortals. One day when the boy was about two, he went with his granddaddy for a ride in the car. This was long before seat belt laws, so Jeff rode standing up in the front seat, with his arm around his grandfather's neck. Suddenly a dog ran right in front of the car. Jeff's grandfather grabbed him at the same time he slammed on the brakes, but he could not break the boy's fall entirely. Jeff's forehead smacked the dashboard just hard enough to smart, which set him off on a good five-minute howl. Once he had caught his breath enough to speak, he looked through his wet eyelashes at his beloved grandfather, and said, "Paw-paw, what did I do wrong?"

It is a story that always makes me want to sit down for a little cry of my own, because that child's loss of innocence is something we all have to suffer. We get through two or ten or twenty years of our lives believing in a universe that rewards good and punishes evil, until one day life slams on the brakes and we learn the truth: you can do everything right and still get hurt. Goodness is no protection from pain.

> *You can do everything right and still get hurt. Goodness is no protection from pain.*

If life teaches us that core truth, our faith confirms it. Jesus was as good as good gets, and still he suffered pain—all kinds of pain—not only physical pain but also spiritual pain and emotional pain. By facing into it instead of running away from it, he showed us a stunning new way to live, but few of us have followed. In spite of everything he said and did, most of us still cling to our own version of the truth: namely, that if we are very, very good, God won't let anything bad happen to us. We will be protected. We will be spared. It is a great perversion of the gospel, but it is also very human, as human as Peter's response when Jesus broke the bad news to his disciples for the first time.

He was going to die, he told them, and it was going to be awful: bloody, painful, humiliating. He did not want them to be fooled, however. When the time came, they were not to believe Jesus' death was some horrible mistake that should have been avoided. They were to believe that God was in it, working to turn his hurt flesh into a body that would last forever.

That was what he wanted them to know, but Peter heard only the first part, the suffering and death part, before he exploded. "God forbid it, Lord! This must never happen to you!" It is hard to tell what was going on inside Peter's head. Plenty of people say he was putting his own agenda ahead of God's and that he should never, ever have used God's name to challenge God's will. My own interpretation is simpler. I just think he loved Jesus and did not want him to die. I also think death was the worst fear Peter had, and that Jesus' reference to his own death cranked Peter's fear up so high he could not stand it.

"God forbid it, Lord! This must never happen to you!" Why? Because if it can happen to you it can happen to me. It can happen to anyone, and no one is safe. If Jesus was vulnerable, then so was everyone else. That was what Peter was protesting, strongly, but Jesus' response to him was just as strong. "Get behind me, Satan! You are a stumbling block to me; for you are setting your mind not on divine things but on human things."

It is the harshest rebuke Jesus gives anyone in all the Gospels, but his use of the word "Satan" lets us know just how tempted he was. Peter's suggestion that he should be spared matched something inside of him. He would pray the same thing himself before he died ("My Father, if it is possible, let this cup pass from me"), but meanwhile God had given him a vision of his death that was not all dark.

It leaked light. There was clearly something that lay beyond it, and he knew his job was to walk toward it instead of running away.

It is the harshest rebuke Jesus gives anyone in all the Gospels.

It was a vision he tried to share with his disciples, by daring them to follow him. If they were not afraid to lose their lives, he told them, they might be surprised to find them. The image he used was a cross, which had no religious meaning at that time, since Jesus had not yet died on one. A cross was simply the method of execution preferred by the Roman government. It struck fear into people's hearts the same way an electric chair or a lethal injection strikes fear into ours.

There were days when the road to Jerusalem was lined with crosses, each of them bearing the dead or dying body of someone whose public execution was meant to scare everyone who saw it. Crucifixion was not only a very efficient form of punishment, it was also a very effective form of intimidation. It reinforced the idea that death was the most awful thing in the world and that people with any sense should do everything in their power to avoid it.

By telling his disciples to pick up their crosses, Jesus defied that idea. He suggested that there were worse things than death in the world, and that living in fear was near the top of the list. If they were going to let fear run their lives, then fear would become their god. The only standard for their behavior would become how much something scared them or not. If it did not scare them, they would do it. If it did scare them, they would not do it. And when their anxious days finally came to an end (death cannot be avoided forever, after all), they would discover that they had never really lived at all.

But that was not the only choice they had. Instead of surrendering themselves to their fear, they could surrender themselves to God. They could deny the panic-stricken voice inside of them—the one that kept ordering them to play it safe—and listen for that other voice instead, the one that says, "Wake up. Follow me. Do not fear." That voice has never promised safety. It has always promised life. It has never offered freedom from pain. It has only offered freedom from fear.

I do not believe we all have to go get ourselves killed in order to follow Jesus. Some people have. We call them saints. But God seems to allow the rest of us a broader understanding of the cross than that. In Luke, Jesus tells his followers to take up their crosses daily (9:23), which sounds more like a way of life than a death wish. He does not tell them to go find their crosses, either, because he is pretty sure they already know right where they are. He just encourages them to go ahead and pick the wretched things up—to stop covering them up and tripping over them and pretending they are not there. He urges them to squat down and get hold of them so they can find out for themselves that there is more to life than being afraid of death.

Two thousand years later, our own crosses do not have much to do with standing up to the Roman government. But fear is timeless, and my guess is that each of us has something of which we are deathly afraid. Maybe it is the fear of admitting an addiction that is eating away at your life. Or maybe it is the fear of tackling a memory that still has the power to suck the breath right out of you. Maybe it is the fear of standing up for something you believe in, or telling the truth about who you are to people who are going to damn you for it. Maybe it is the fear of discovering you have an illness that no medicine can cure, or that your child does, or your friend.

Whatever it is that scares you to death, so that you start offering to do anything, anything at all, if it will just go away—that is your cross, and if you leave it lying there it will kill you. If you turn away from it (God forbid it, Lord!) with the excuse that this should never have happened to you, then you deny God the chance to show you the greatest mystery of them all: that there, right there in the dark fist of your worst fear, is the door to abundant life.

> *There, right there in the dark fist of your worst fear, is the door to abundant life.*

I cannot say more than that. I don't dare, or God might test me on it, but Jesus does dare. Stop running from your cross, he says. Reach down and pick it up. It isn't nearly as scary once you get your hands on it, and no one is asking you to handle it alone. All you have to do is believe in God more than you believe in your fear. Then pick it up, come on with me, and I will show you the way to the door. Amen.

Chapter Ten

Unless a Grain Falls

| John 12:20-33 |

LAST WEEK A WOMAN CAME TO SEE ME for some help with her power bill. After I handed her the check, she said, "What kind of church is this, anyway?" I told her it was an Episcopal church, which did not appear to help her any. "I never heard of that before," she said. "What do y'all believe?" I started to tell her, but she had specific things in mind. "Do you believe you have to be saved?" she asked me. While I was trying to decide whether to give her the long answer or the short answer, she said, "Let me put it this way: Do you believe Jesus died for your sins?"

"Of course," I said, and while she still looked a little sorry for me, as if she knew I was saying something I did not fully understand, she decided to let me pass. "Well, so do I," she said, tucked the check in her pocketbook, and left.

That was the end of it for her, but not for me. By asking me about the connection between my life and Jesus' death, she opened up all the old uncomfortable questions for me again. Yes, I believe Christ died for the sins of the whole world—only how did that work, exactly? Were they all piled up there at the foot of the cross, sins past and sins to come, and when he breathed his last they simply vanished?

Or was it more like a ledger in the hands of an angry God, with every person's name followed by a long list of debts? Every time God wrote down another one, God said, "Someone is going to have hell to pay for this." Then one day Jesus said, "I will. I'll pay the whole thing," and that was that. God closed the book and threw it in the trash. Only how did something that happened two thousand years ago affect what I may do tomorrow? Does Jesus go on dying for our sins? And what kind of God would require that?

Since Christ's death and resurrection are central to this faith we profess, I think it is extremely important that each of us struggle with what those events mean to us, both as individuals and as a community. It is not enough to repeat what we have been told. If we really believe there is a connection between our lives and Christ's death, then the least we can do is spend some quiet hours asking God to teach us about that.

The twelfth chapter of John contains most of what Jesus had to say about his own death in that Gospel. According to John, he said it in Jerusalem during Passover, the last week of his life, when some Greeks who were in town for the festival asked to see Jesus. Their request was a sign to him that his hour had come.

These were not local people who had heard about him from their neighbors. They were Gentiles from across the sea who wanted to meet the Hebrew holy man. When the authorities heard about it, they would step up their efforts to arrest him. The more famous he became, the more dangerous he was to them. Something had to be done about him, and soon.

"The hour has come for the Son of Man to be glorified," Jesus told them, and not only them but the whole crowd standing around. "Very truly, I tell you, unless a grain of wheat falls to the earth and dies, it remains just a single grain; but if it dies, it bears much fruit," he said.

It is a statement about the redemptive power of suffering, both his and ours, and it is no easier to hear now than it ever was. What he is telling us is that if we do everything in our power to protect our lives the way they are—if we successfully prevent change, prevent conflict, prevent pain—then at the end we will find that we had no life at all. But if we hate our lives in this world, which as far as I am concerned can only mean if we hate all the ways we cheapen our lives by chasing comfort, safety, and superiority in this world—if we hate that enough to stop it and start chasing God instead—then there will be no end to the abundance of our lives.

Those were the two choices he laid out for his listeners, the same two available to him as the net drew in around him. The first way, the way of self-protection, was closed to suffering. If he chose it, he could do a couple of things. He could stop walking around in the open and go underground instead, sleeping in a different hideout each night. Or he could simply tone down his message. That would work too. He could find more pleasant ways to phrase things. He could stop eating with outcasts and start showing more respect for organized religion. If he loved his life and wanted to save it, that is.

If, on the other hand, he loved something more than his life, then there was a second way open to him. Call it the way of self-offering. That way contained not only the possibility but the probability of suffering—not as the main goal but as a by-product of the main goal. If he kept walking around in the open where anyone could get to him, if he kept speaking and living his confrontational message, then eventually he would suffer for it. There were no two ways about it. He was crossing lines of power you do not cross without getting electrocuted. His only choice was whether to cross them or not.

> *He was crossing lines of power you do not cross without getting electrocuted.*

But he did have a choice, which is essential to his story. There are so many kinds of suffering in this world that have nothing to do with the gospel. There is nothing redemptive about famine, genocide, or incest. There is no choice for those who suffer from such things, and no one should have to endure them. The only kind of suffering I am talking about today is the kind Jesus chose—again, not as his goal but as a by-product of his goal—which was to be fully who God had created him to be no matter what it cost.

A grain of wheat cannot grow unless it dies. That is how Jesus put it. If you encase it in plastic and hang it around your neck, it will never be good for anything but a bauble. For the seed to do what it was meant to do, it has to be given up. It has to fall into the earth and be buried. It has to sit down there in the dark until its hour comes, when it will swell, crack, and hatch new life—a green shoot that will climb toward the sun until it breaks through, becoming a golden stalk of wheat that bears much fruit. If you dig around in its roots looking for the seed, you won't find it anymore. It is dead and gone. It gave up its life so there could be more wheat in the world.

This is a very different understanding of Jesus' death than the one most of us were taught, which was that Jesus died to atone for our sins. According to John, Jesus died to fill the world with wheat, with so many sons and daughters of God that no one would ever want for bread again. Only in order to do that, the seed had to be planted. It had to die, or it would never grow.

If Jesus had saved his life, gone on a speaking tour, and written some books, there is no telling how long his movement might have lasted—a hundred years, maybe, or at least until the books fell apart. But because he was willing to lose his life—because his message mattered so much to him that he was willing to show people what it meant instead of just telling them about it—his seed bore much fruit, more than it ever did while he was alive.

Because Jesus was willing to die, God could raise him from the dead. Because Jesus was willing to die, people could discover that death was not the worst thing that could happen to them. Because Jesus was willing to die, a new community could form in his name, one that redefined its life on the basis of his death.

One of the main points in that redefinition was a new view of suffering. It was no longer something to be avoided at all costs, nor did it mean that God was mad at you. It might in fact mean that God loved you very much, because when someone on a path toward God deliberately chooses the self-offering that goes with that path, then suffering becomes one of God's most powerful tools for transforma-tion. It is how God breaks open hard hearts so that they may be made new. It is how God cracks open closed lives so that they can get some air into them again.

When Jesus died, this power was made manifest. By absorbing into himself the worst that the world could do to a child of God and by refusing to do any of it back, he made sure it was put to death with him. By suffering every kind of hurt and shame without ever once letting them deflect him from his purpose, he broke their hold on humankind. In him, sin met its match. He showed us what is possible. These are just some of the fruits of Christ's death, things that could never have happened if he had not been willing to fall to the ground.

Each of us has a grain of wheat with which to cast our votes.

So here we sit, the local field of wheat who owe our lives to him. If he had not died, we would not be here. Because he did, we are. He has spoken to us about the way of life and the way of death, letting us know that these are the only two choices and that none of us may abstain. When the hour comes, each of us has a grain of wheat with which to cast our votes. It is the grain of our lives, and all of creation is holding its breath to see what we will do with it. Amen.

Chapter Eleven

The Dress Rehearsal

John 11:1-44

YOU CAN STILL VISIT LAZARUS'S TOMB IN Bethany. It is a little ways up from the church that bears his name. You just go out the front door, turn left up the steep cobblestone road, and look for the Lazarus souvenir and gift shop on the right. Directly across the street you can see the entrance to the cave, enclosed by metal railings. For a small fee, you can walk down the winding steps into the wet cellar where the old grave site is—a small round opening in a rock wall, down around knee level. You have to bend almost double to get in, and coming out requires real gymnastic ability. There is only one way to do it: head first, with your upper body already out while your feet are still finding the three small steps—looking up as you straighten up, trying not to scrape your back. If it really is Lazarus's tomb, then he did not come out of it like a man walking out of prison. He came out of it like a baby being born again—first his poor wrapped face, then his bandaged hands, and finally his feet.

It must have been absolutely terrifying for him and for everyone else—everyone but Jesus, that is—who seems to know how everything is going to turn out from the moment he first learns that Lazarus is ill. The news reaches him right after he has escaped a religious death squad in Jerusalem. He is safe across the River Jordan (about thirty miles away) when Martha and Mary send word to him that their brother is ill.

Lazarus and his sisters are three of Jesus' best friends. They want him to come right away, but he does not. He waits two whole days, which is hard to imagine, and then he travels a day or two more, so that by the time he arrives in Bethany he has missed the funeral by four days. This is not news to him, however. He knew it before he ever set out, and does not seem very worried about it, but his confidence is wasted on Martha.

"Lord," she says to him, "if you had been here, my brother would not have died." There is such love in that greeting, and such blame. She knows Jesus is a life-saver, only where was he when she needed him? She and Mary have just buried Lazarus way before his time with no help from their dearest friend, and any of you who have lost a loved one know what she is going through. "If only I had made him go to the doctor sooner." "If only I had not left her alone." When you lose someone you love, you can drive yourself crazy thinking of all the ways it might have been avoided ("If only . . ."). For Martha, Jesus is the one who could have made the difference, only he was not there and now it is too late.

> **There is such love in that greeting, and such blame.**

At least she thinks it is too late. She is also willing to believe that it might not be, although this possibility is beyond her imagining. "Lord, if you had been here, my brother would not have died. But even now I know that God will give you whatever you ask of him." Then she and Jesus have a short, powerful exchange about resurrection, in which Martha talks about it as something that happens in the future and Jesus talks about it as something that happens right now—resurrection and life for anyone who believes in him.

We have heard this so often that many of us are numb to it. The basic idea, as most of us were taught it, is that those who accept Jesus as Lord receive a coupon for eternal life. Later on, when we need it, we can present it to the angel of death and gain entrance into the land of light and life. In the meantime, all we have to do to secure our reward is to believe in Jesus and act as though we do.

You can hear some of that in what Martha says. When Jesus tells her that her brother will rise again, she says, "I know that he will rise again in the resurrection on the last day." But Jesus corrects her, and here I want to use the other word for the Greek word *pisteuo*, which can mean either "trust" or "believe."

"I am the resurrection and the life," Jesus says. "Those who trust in me, even though they die, will live, and everyone who lives and trusts in me will never die. Do you trust this?" (John 11:25-26; author's alteration).

He does not say he has power to give resurrection and life. He says that he *is* those things, that in his presence they become present reality, because he is one with the Great I Am, whose life is indestructible. Those who hook up with him will never die, no matter what happens to their bodies, because he is hooked up with the source and sustainer of all life. Those who trust that with him—in him—begin their eternal lives right now, and nothing on earth can snuff them out.

> *He does not say he has power to give resurrection and life.*
> *He says that he is those things.*

This is very different from the promise of a future reward, and it is what Jesus is about to do with Lazarus. He is about to prove that Lazarus is alive and well, even though his body has lain four days in a tomb. He is about to call his beloved friend back from the living heart of God so that those who think he is dead can think again.

But first Jesus must repeat this whole scene with Mary, who says the same thing her sister does. "Lord, if you had been here, my brother would not have died." Please note that everyone in this story is focused on preventing death, while Jesus is focused on outliving it. When he sees Mary weeping and those who are with her also weeping, it tears him up inside. "He was greatly disturbed in spirit and deeply moved," John writes, but the Greek is more visceral than that.

Jesus snorts. His bowels turn over inside of him, and when those present offer to show him where Lazarus has been laid to rest, he weeps—but again, two different words here. Mary and the others are wailing out loud. Jesus sheds tears. Because he is sad about Lazarus, certainly. But also because everyone else is wailing. They have given up on Lazarus. They have all said good-bye to him, and they think Jesus has come to do the same thing. As many times as he has told them, they still do not get it. It never occurs to them that Jesus might have come to say hello instead.

Like any good teacher, he decides to show them what he means instead of telling them again. After thanking God for what is about to happen, he shouts, "Lazarus, come out!" and Lazarus does, trailing his bandages behind him like a scarf he no longer needs.

Until a few days ago, I always thought this was a story about something Jesus did *to* Lazarus—Lazarus being the prop, almost, the empty shell that Jesus pumped full of life again. But now I think it is a story about something Jesus did *with* Lazarus—who was, after all, his beloved friend—who did trust in him and who was therefore full of God's own life. He had moved on, certainly. The body he left behind had already begun to stink, and he was presumably napping in the bosom of Abraham when he heard his friend (who was also his Lord) cry, "Lazarus, come out!"

Because they loved each other, Lazarus did. He crawled back through the dark tunnel toward the sound of that voice and emerged, blinking and stumbling, into the light—which was less bright than the light where he had come from, but which was God's light just the same because Jesus was there, smiling through his tears. Then his sisters fell all over him, and his neighbors stood back clutching each other as if they had seen a ghost, and when the religious death squad back in Jerusalem heard about it they stepped up their efforts to assassinate Jesus, which would very soon succeed.

So Jesus traded his life for Lazarus's life, among others, by doing with his friend what God was about to do with him. The timing is important. The next death we will hear about is Jesus' own, which will be scarier and stink far worse than Lazarus's did, and I believe we are given this story as a kind of dress rehearsal. Whether or not you can accept it as actual fact is beside the point, I think. It is the truth in it we are given to trust.

So Jesus traded his life for Lazarus's life, among others, by doing with his friend what God was about to do with him.

"I am the resurrection and the life," he says. Not later but right now. We can hook up with that life while we live, so that eternal life is not something we are waiting for at the end of time but something we begin living right now, because we trust in him who lived it and lives it and invites us to live it with him, world without end. Amen.

Chapter Twelve

Surviving Crucifixion

ONE SUMMER, I HAD TWO PET spiders at home in my kitchen. They were small, black, and furry with red dots on their backs. They played chase on the water faucet and hid from each other in the African violet. They provided early morning entertainment and they presumably ate bugs, so I was glad to have them. Imagine my distress, then, when I found one of them belly up on the windowsill with all his legs curled up. A jar lid had fallen on him and his thorax was crushed. I turned him over with a toothpick and let him lie in state there in the sun.

A week later, he looked plumper for some reason. A couple of days after that, his legs uncurled. The next week I lifted one of his legs with a toothpick and he pulled it back, just slightly. He was definitely alive again, although not the way he had been. Do spiders hibernate? Do they regenerate, like starfish who lose an arm? I don't know. All I know is that my husband and I were both unnerved by his new life.

"That spider was *dead*," Ed said to me. "This is definitely creepy." Why? Because in the normal course of events, what is dead stays dead. And if it comes back to life again, that is because it was not dead after all. There was a spark of life left in it that was breathed on and brought back to life, so that death was pushed away for a little while longer. And that is miracle enough for most of us.

A resurrection is a miracle of another order. There is no continuity with life as we know it. The spark is utterly extinguished. The heart stops. The legs curl up for good. Death occurs, beyond a shadow of a doubt. The living withdraw to get on with their lives and the silence is complete. Then, when everything is over, something entirely new begins. What was cold becomes warm again, and what lay still sits up. Creation occurs all over again—not a spark rescued from the ashes but a whole new fire kindled out of nothing—the gracious act of the only one who can make life out of dust, not just once upon a time, or even at the end of time, but over and over again.

If we do not believe this, Paul says, we are of all people most to be pitied, and yet the resurrection of the dead in general and the bodily resurrection of Jesus in particular are hard for many believers to swallow. Perfectly faithful people say that it really does not matter to them whether it happened or not, that if Jesus' body was stolen and he was quietly buried by his friends, they would still do their best to live by his teachings. Others say it was the survival of his spirit that mattered, and that too much thinking about what happens after you die can distract you from what you are supposed to be doing while you are alive.

The truth of the matter, for me, is that resurrection is nothing any of us has ever seen or experienced for ourselves. Near-death experiences, yes; ghostly visitations, yes; but none of us knows firsthand what it is like to be resurrected from the dead. According to the Bible, God set it up that way. Hundreds of people witnessed Jesus' crucifixion, but not one living soul was there when he was raised from the dead. The women saw him afterward, when he was back on his feet, and his disciples saw him after that, although not for long, but no one was allowed the privilege of seeing him come back to life.

> *Resurrection is nothing any of us has ever seen or experienced for ourselves.*

So none of us should feel too badly about finding it hard to believe. Resurrection is not something we can test, like gravity or true north. It is a nonmaterial reality, which was one of the reasons Paul was pushing it so hard on the Corinthians. They were champion materialists—big eaters and drinkers, with big appetites in all departments—who preferred religious truths with immediate results. Any-thing that happened outside their day-to-day experience was not of much interest to them. They preferred to go for all the gusto they could get and leave the dead to bury the dead.

> *Resurrection is not something we can test,*
> *like gravity or true north.*

By pushing them on resurrection, Paul was pushing them to believe that life was more than they could see, taste, or feel. He wanted them to know that there was a dimension and quality of life that was all but invisible to them—something much more compre-hensive than the present—and that if they missed out on it then they were the most pitiful people on earth. If he would not let up on it, it was because he was driven by his own experience of Christ's resur-rection—a flash of light on the road to Damascus, a voice that came out of nowhere—a complete transformation of his life by someone who was supposed to be dead and gone.

Paul learned everything he needed to know about resurrection in that one blinding moment: that God has power beyond all human understanding, that life is stronger than death, that none of us can ever say for sure that everything is over for us. If God can raise the dead—and, just as important, if we *believe* God can raise the dead—then our despair will be temporary and our hope invincible, not because we know how to keep it alive but because God has never forgotten how to breathe life into piles of dust.

We do not know what resurrection will mean for us in the end. We cannot know how it will feel or work or look. But we do have evidence it is so. God has woven resurrection into our daily lives so that we can learn the shape of it and perhaps learn to trust the strength of it when our own times come.

> *God has woven resurrection into our daily lives so that we*
> *can learn the shape of it and perhaps learn to trust the*
> *strength of it when our own times come.*

I am thinking of a friend of mine, a teacher, who was fired from his job six months short of his retirement after twenty-five years. It was a nasty piece of work on the part of his superiors. They wanted to punish him for challenging them, and to make him an example for anyone else thinking about trying the same thing. They called it early retirement and gave him a party he suffered through. "I've been to my own funeral," he said weeks later, recounting the pain of it. "I lost my students, my program, my livelihood, my pride. But you know what? There really is life after death. I'm doing things I always wanted to do but never had time. I'm spending time with my wife. I'm finding energy I thought I had lost forever. Getting crucified turned out better than I thought."

I am thinking of Saint James's Church in Richmond, which burned in 1994. Established in the 1700s, it was one of the oldest churches in the city when lightning struck the steeple during a summer thunderstorm. Before anyone could respond, everything burned up: the pews, the prayer books, the organ, the altar. The next Sunday was baptism Sunday, and do you know what those people did? They put up tents in the street and baptized babies while they stood in the ashes of their ruined church. A sign maker in town donated a banner that has become that church's motto: "Let Us Rise Up and Build," it says (Nehemiah 2:18).

I am thinking of another friend of mine who was diagnosed with Lou Gehrig's disease in her fifties and who surprised everyone around her by growing more and more alive as she died. Her nervous system quit on her, inch by inch. After she lost her ability to speak, she took up watercoloring. She made everyone who visited her watercolor too, and she posted our creations on her kitchen wall as though they were masterpieces of the world. She continued team-teaching weekend workshops on faith in life although she could communicate only by writing on the board. No, I take that back. She communicated also with her wide-open, lit-up face. When she died, surrounded by her friends, she was as alive as anyone I have ever known.

These are not resurrection stories, because nobody knows about that but God. And yet they are true stories about the raising of the dead, much more impressive than my spider—people who are laid low and by all rights should never rise again who suddenly sit up in their ashes, brush themselves off, and go on to live more than they ever lived before.

> *It is how God works, now and forever—not by protecting us from death but by bringing us back to life again—because life, not death, is God's will for us.*

It is entirely unnatural. It is how God works, now and forever—not by protecting us from death but by bringing us back to life again—because life, not death, is God's will for us. Every moment of our lives carries the seeds of that truth. Those who miss it are of all people most to be pitied. And those who believe it? Our hope shall never die. Amen.

Chapter Thirteen

Portents and Signs

Luke 21:5-19

AS THE END OF THE PRESENT MILLEN-nium draws near, stranger and stranger things happen. Survivalists take to the woods with their stockpiles of weapons. More passive types commit mass suicide in hopes of escaping to another planet. Even the most placid among us have been known to check the sky from time to time, just to make sure everything is where it is supposed to be.

It is easy enough to see why some people think history is drawing to a close. All you have to do is hold a newspaper in one hand and Luke's Gospel in the other. "Nation will rise against nation, and kingdom against kingdom." Check. "There will be great earth-quakes." Check. "In various places famines and plagues." Check, check. "Dreadful portents and great signs from heaven." Does a gaping hole in the ozone layer count? Check.

"They will arrest you and persecute you." Well, no, not yet, or at least not here. In Central America, yes, in South Africa, maybe, as well as in the Middle East; but it is hard to read the part about being brought before kings and governors without thinking of the second-century church, and the third, for whom martyrdom was a fact of daily life. Church history began with those who were burned at the stake or beheaded or fed to the lions.

So this frightening passage not only looks forward; it also looks back, to the many times before now when Christians experienced all these things and believed their world was coming to an end, only it did not. This inexplicable delay in the coming of the Lord is one of the stickiest problems the Christian church has ever had to face. Jesus himself did not seem to know the answer. "Truly, I tell you, this generation will not pass away until all things have taken place," he said, almost two thousand years ago (Luke 21:32).

> **This inexplicable delay in the coming of the Lord is one of the stickiest problems the Christian church has ever had to face.**

He says it as part of his last public teaching on earth. He has done everything he knows how to do. He has said everything he knows how to say. He has come to Jerusalem knowing full well he will collide with the authorities there, and he is sitting in the temple talking with his disciples when some of them begin to admire the place out loud, commenting on how beautiful the stone is, how grand the gifts dedicated to God, when Jesus reminds them that it will all be rubble some day soon.

He does not say it to be cruel. He is simply telling them the truth—that the things of this world will not last—that even some place as stunning and holy as the temple will become a ruin when the old world collapses in upon itself, which is becoming as clear to him as his own death. It is the kind of news that shrinks your heart and ties your stomach in knots. It is the kind of news that makes you start collecting canned goods in the basement and looking around for someone who can save you—someone who seems to have access to God's calendar and who will tell you exactly when the ship starts to sink so that you can make it to the lifeboats in time.

Only Jesus does not recommend that course of action. He warns against it, in fact. "Beware that you are not led astray," he tells those gathered around him; "for many will come in my name and say, 'I am he!' and 'The time is near!' Do not go after them. When you hear of wars and insurrections, do not be terrified; for these things must take place first, but the end will not follow immediately."

Do not go after them. Do not be terrified. When the sky is falling? When the world is coming to an end? That is right. Do not go after them. Do not be terrified.

I will tell you the most interesting thing about this passage for me. When I read the newspaper or tune into the five o'clock news on the radio—when I hear of wars and insurrections, and holes in the ozone layer, and rising interest rates, and unemployment figures, and all the other symptoms of a world in deep distress, I start wondering where God has gone. I wonder if God had something important to do in some other corner of the universe and forgot about us here, or just got tired of bailing us out and decided to let the human experiment come to an end.

I read the signs of the times as signs of God's absence, in other words, but according to Luke's Gospel they are not signs of God's absence at all but signs of God's sure and certain presence. Nothing is going on that is unknown to God—not the things in the newspaper or the things in our own lives; God foresaw them long ago and encouraged us not to be terrified. Because to become terrified is to become part of the problem, you see, which is not what God has in mind for us. God has something else in mind for us, something Jesus calls endurance.

> I read the signs of the times as signs of God's absence, in other words, but according to Luke's Gospel they are not signs of God's absence at all but signs of God's sure and certain presence.

These things happen, he said. *These things must take place. When all that is lovely to you, when all that is holy looks as if it may soon be reduced to rubble, do not lose heart. I never promised to lead you around the trouble in the world; I only promised to lead you through. Do not be terrified, little flock. Hold on to one another and follow me through. Not a hair of your head will perish, not ultimately. By your endurance you will gain your souls.*

According to the newspaper, the mainline church is one of the many things in the world that is falling apart. We read that we are losing members. We read that we are torn by schism and scandal, and that it is hard to tell what the church stands for anymore. With all of this in mind, I and several members of the congregation recently attended the annual meeting of our denomination in Atlanta. We went to remember that we are not a solitary outpost of believers in northeast Georgia but that we are connected to a worldwide communion of faith who remember us when they say their prayers the same way we remember them. We went to take our places in the greater body of Christ of which we are all a part, and some of us went with concerns about the health of that body.

Our presiding bishop was with us, and we spent all day Saturday talking with him about the issues confronting the church and the world: the hamstrung economy, family values, human sexuality, the growing number of poor people, the challenges faced by our youth. We talked honestly and from the heart. We expressed vast differences. We listened carefully to one another. No one booed anyone else, and there was a lot of applause. A sense of mutual respect for one another pervaded our long day of dialogue—perhaps because we prayed together morning, noon, and night—and I think it is fair to say that we all came away with a sense that God was with us, and is with us, in all our differences and struggle.

There is a time-honored saying in the Anglican church, that schism is worse than heresy. What that means is that it is okay for us to disagree, and it is even okay for some of us to be way, way out of line as far as orthodox theology is concerned, but what is not okay is for us to let go of one another. Staying in communion with one another—holding on to one another through all the stormy blasts that blow us around—that is how we know that God is still with us, no matter what the headlines say. Come earthquakes, come famines, come plagues, come great signs from heaven, we are to hold on to one another—we are to endure in that—because holding on to one another is how we hold on to our Lord.

> Come earthquakes, come famines, come plagues, come great signs from heaven, we are to hold on to one another.

I had a very wonderful old lady for a friend until she died several years ago at the age of ninety-seven. The newspaper headlines changed a lot over the course of her lifetime. When she was born, in 1894, there were no airplanes, no televisions, no automobiles to speak of. Russia was ruled by a czar and China by an emperor. The only way to get to Europe was by boat.

As she got older, her short-term memory got worse, but her long-term memory got better, and one day as I sat by her bed she told me about a summer's day from her childhood, when she and some of her girlfriends hitched up their long skirts and climbed Mount Washington in the White Mountains of New Hampshire. They went too far and stayed too long, she said, and before they knew it the beautiful sunset they were watching had turned into a foggy dusk so that they could not see their hands in front of their faces.

No one had a flashlight—flashlights had not been invented yet—and no one knew for sure which way was down, but they agreed they would all hold hands and that they would not, under any circumstance, let go of one another. So that is how they did it—one girl at the front, picking her way down the mountain one step at a time—and all the rest of them strung out behind her, holding onto each other's wrists so that they made a living human chain. Every now and then someone would want to argue about which way to go and the others would listen, but what none of them did was let go.

"Sometimes," my friend said, "all I knew or could see of the world was the hand ahead of me and the one behind. Sometimes my arms ached so badly I thought I would cry out loud, but that is how we made it at last. We found our way home by holding on to one another."

Do not be terrified, he said, *for all these things must take place. But lo, I am with you always, even unto the end of the age.* Amen.

Chapter Fourteen

The Delivery Room

Luke 21:20-28

EVER SO OFTEN, WE GET A STRONG reminder that the ways of God are not the ways of the world. According to the ways of the world, Christmas is lighten-up time—one month out of twelve when we give ourselves permission to go to parties on week nights and buy children's toys and decorate our homes like parade floats. It is the season of eggnog, evergreen, and peppermint, when the instinct to purchase is hallowed and overeating is required. Whatever else may be going on in the world, Christmas is a time to rise above it—to be happy, to be at peace, to anticipate birth.

The ways of God are less cheerful, overall. They offer us no shortcuts to joy. If the church calendar is any indication, things always get darker before they get light. However much we would like to take a taxi straight to Christmas, there are these dark days of Advent to go through first—on foot—down a road that leads through a graveyard, through the wilderness, through a river of repentance. There is a lot of waiting along the way, waiting and telling the truth about all the scary things that can happen before the birth of real joy takes place.

However much we would like to take a taxi straight to Christmas, there are these dark days of Advent to go through first.

If we decline to take this road, which we are free to do, then Christmas becomes little more than a lovely parachute. It will work for a while to keep our feet off the ground but come January 1 it will land, covering the same old landscape with a thin skin of colorful spent silk. God knows. The old world must end, in some fashion or another, before the new world can begin. If you have lived through it yourself, then you know too that you cannot get well until you admit you are sick, that you cannot put your life back together again until you stop pretending it is not broken, that you cannot find your new beginning until you say out loud, to anyone who will listen, that you have come to the end of your rope.

What is true for us on an individual level is true for the whole cosmos. That is what Jesus tells those who are standing around him in the temple near the end of his own life. The days of vengeance are coming, he tells them. Things will get bad, very bad, but they are not to fear. They are to hold their heads up high, because their redemption is drawing near.

The people of God have been listening to Jesus say this for a long time now. They may listen to him say it for a long time to come, but I think his words have particular punch today, as we approach the year 2000. In the history of the world, not a lot of people have gotten to see three zeros in the date on New Year's Day. It will be a great privilege for those of us who do—if we can survive the anxiety, that is. I don't know why zeros get people all excited, but they do, whether it is the candles on a cake they are counting or the miles on an odometer or the dawn of a new millennium. Maybe zeros impress us with how much time has really passed, or maybe it is the symmetry that worries us—that if God likes round numbers, for instance, ours may get called.

I remember buying a huge piece of newsprint once, when I was cramming for a history exam. It must have been six feet long. First I measured to the center of it and put a zero there, for the dividing line between the time before Christ and the time after. Then I went all the way down to the bottom of the sheet and started writing down the earliest events in biblical history, like God's promise to Abraham and the exodus from Egypt.

I won't lead you all the way through, but by the time I got to World War I and Vatican II, I looked up and realized I was out of paper. Or, to put it more accurately, I was out of time. I looked way down the sheet where history began about two thousand years before Christ and I looked at where I was about two thousand years after Christ and I thought, "Uh-oh. I hope God's got some more paper on hand."

We are not the first generation to wonder if the end is near. It happens whenever the known world falls apart—when governments collapse and famine sweeps the land, when rivers run with blood and whole nations crumble under the weight of their eroded values. The prophet Daniel thought it was happening in his day. Jesus thought it was happening in his, and Luke thought the same thing when he wrote his Gospel.

In the forty or so years since Jesus' death, things had gotten much worse for Luke and his church. Peter and Paul had been executed. The emperor Nero had taken to setting Christians on fire to use as garden torches at his palace parties. Then Israel rebelled against Rome, and Jerusalem became a battlefield until Titus demolished it in A.D. 70. The temple was destroyed, over a million people died, and another ninety-seven thousand were taken captive. Masada fell three years later and Vesuvius erupted in A.D. 79. Jesus' words came as no surprise to Luke's congregation, who recognized themselves in what he said. "People will faint from fear and foreboding of what is coming upon the world, for the powers of the heavens will be shaken."

> *We are not the first generation to wonder if the end is near. It happens whenever the known world falls apart.*

That was the first century. We are about to enter the twenty-first with some fear and foreboding of our own. There is still war in Jerusalem, not to mention eastern Europe and Africa. We have gotten used to death tolls in the millions and natural disasters that take our breath away. The hardest part is the children. They are dying every second, and those who are not dying are learning from us what it takes to survive: a gang, a gun, a drug to ease the pain.

A few weeks ago I found out that homicide is the number two cause of violent death among teenagers in Georgia, right between car wrecks and suicide. Between 1979 and 1991 almost fifty thousand American children were killed by guns—a death toll higher than that of the war in Vietnam. In a 1990 survey, almost 50 percent of white teenagers and 40 percent of their black classmates had carried a weapon to school in the past thirty days. And that is not all. In

Georgia, 29 percent of first babies are born to mothers under twenty. A quarter of those mothers do not have high school diplomas, and more than a third are unmarried. Over half of the people living in Atlanta housing projects are under the age of seventeen. I don't know what the figures are where you live, but I'll bet they are similar.

Someone just told me a story about a friend of his who met a nine-year-old boy living in an inner-city neighborhood. Trying to make conversation with the boy, he asked a standard question. "What do you want to be when you grow up?" he asked the boy, who gave him a non-standard answer.

"If I grow up," the boy said, "I think I might want to be a fireman." His two older brothers had already been killed in drive-by shootings, he explained, so he wasn't going to get his hopes up. "If I grow up . . . "

Whenever things get this bad, people of faith generally start pounding on God's door. "Where are you?" they shout. "And when are you coming back? We need you here *right now.*" Those are the people who were standing around Jesus in the temple that day, the people who were sitting in Luke's congregation hoping for some answers. There may even be some sitting right here. I know I am one of them, when things get really bad. When I feel faint from fear and foreboding at what is coming upon the world, I want a map with a red star on it that says, "You are here." I want to know the plan and where I can go to stay safe, only Jesus won't help. "Stand up and raise your heads," he says, "because your redemption is drawing near."

Like so much of the gospel, this goes against human nature in a big way. The normal reaction to disaster is to cover your head and find some place to hide. Jesus suggests that we stay right where we are and look up instead—because something big is coming, something we won't want to miss. If you ask me, this is a major fork in the road of human belief, with God's ways going off in one direction and the ways of the world going off in another. It is the hardest decision any of us will ever make—to stick with our own interpretation of events or to open ourselves up to God's interpretation. In order to make that decision, we may have to re-think God's sovereignty in times like these. We may have to admit that if there is a plan we cannot see it—or if this is it, we do not like it. This is not how we would run the world, only no one asked us. We are not in charge here and never have been. If we have any power at all, it is the power to decide what we will believe and how we will act in the face of things we do not understand.

We can hide from this pain, these cosmic contractions. We can call them chance, fate, chaos, God's absence. Or we can call them God's presence, if we dare, as terrible and inexplicable as that may sound. We can call them birth pangs instead of death throes, and we can volunteer our services in the delivery room. If we let the blood and the screaming scare us off, then we deserve what we get. You cannot change your mind once the baby is on the way. All you can do is trust God while the whole world goes head first down the squeezing black tunnel and pray, pray, that what is born survives.

My opinion is that those of us who yearn for maps and plans are really yearning to be excused from the delivery room. We want to know what the last warning signal will be so that we can go do something else until it is time. We do not want to get ready until we have to, and, all things being equal, we would rather meet the baby after it has been cleaned up and dressed in something soft that smells of talcum powder.

Only Jesus will not cooperate. *Stand up*, he says; *raise your heads.* Attend this birth. It may be able to happen without us, but whatever is waiting to be born in us will not happen, not completely, if we are not there. False prophets sound false alarms. False messiahs peddle false comforts. The true Christ offers us nothing but full participation. He sends us out for hot water, clean towels, something sharp to cut the cord. The rules do not change in frightening times; they just get clearer. The proper response to disaster is to keep loving God and our neighbors as ourselves. The proper posture is to raise our heads. God may have some more paper on hand and God may not. Either way, our calling is the same: to assist God in the deliverance of the world any and every way we can.

> *The proper response to disaster is to keep loving God and our neighbors as ourselves. The proper posture is to raise our heads.*

Someone gave me a cartoon of a street preacher with a sign around his neck that said, "The world is not coming to an end; therefore you must suffer along and learn to cope." A collect in the old prayer book put it like this:

Eternal God, who commits to us the swift and solemn trust of life; since we do not know what a day may bring forth, but only that the hour for serving you is always present, may we wake to the instant claims of your holy will, not waiting for tomorrow, but yielding today. Amen.

PART II

Pain of Death

Chapter Fifteen

Believing What We Cannot Understand

John 19:1-3

ACCORDING TO THOSE WHO calculate such things, it was probably on April 7, A.D. 30, that Jeshua ben Joseph— Jesus, son of Joseph—a teacher from Nazareth, was crucified outside the walls of Jerusalem. It was springtime in Judea; the olive trees were in bloom and the hills to the west of the city were turning green. In the garden of Gethsemane, the first flowers were pushing up through the earth and pollen covered everything like fine gold dust. The birds sang and the breeze blew and the air smelled sweet as the world came to life, but up on Golgotha, from noon until three, something was dying.

Three men hung there on rough wooden crosses, two common thieves and one puzzling revolutionary with a sign above his head: "Jesus of Nazareth," it said in three different languages, "the King of the Jews." It was a joke. It was the truth. It was the charge for which he had been sentenced to die. Different groups of people stood around the feet of the three crosses. There were the relatives of the convicts, and especially the women who loved them. There were a few of the chief priests and Roman functionaries who had been

---

Chapters 15, 16, and 17 were preached at the same Good Friday service.

involved in the trial, present to see that justice was done. And there were a few onlookers who knew no one and whom no one knew, voyeurs who could not resist the occasional execution.

The soldiers were the only ones making any real noise. They were used to it, after all. They were just doing their jobs, and like death row prison guards or orderlies at the morgue, they had long since lost their squeamishness about their work. The hard part was getting the convicts up on the crosses—that part was heavy, sweaty work—but after it was over all they had to do was wait, and they gambled to pass the time, gambled and told bawdy stories that took their minds off their work and made them laugh out loud.

But otherwise it was quiet, a silence punctuated by the clicking of insects, the labored breathing of the criminals, and every now and then a shrill cry from one of the birds of prey circling overhead. It was a death watch, and down on the ground everyone was doing what people do on such occasions. They were thinking about the lives of the people who were dying in front of them, remembering the good times and lamenting the times when things went wrong. They were trying to find the meaning in all those times and they were thinking about their own lives too, their own lives and their own deaths and where God—if they believed in God—where God was in the midst of it all.

> It was a death watch, and down on the ground everyone was doing what people do on such occasions.

That was Good Friday then, and it is Good Friday now—the day on which we stand in front of the cross with our burning eyes and dry mouths and look at it, just look at it. There is no figuring it out. There is no explaining it. There is nothing much to say about it at all. This is the day that God was silent all day long, although the whole world got down on its knees and begged God to speak, to act. Silence was God's answer, and silence marks this day, a day on which we sit or stand or kneel before the cross, most of us knowing what we have been taught to believe about it but feeling something else—trying to reconcile the theological event with the human one—seeing the body of Christ one moment and the corpse of Jesus the next, like one of those trick pictures that change as you move them back and forth. First it is a picture of Christ's triumph on the cross, his victory over sin and death and all the powers that be; but shift it just a little and it is a picture of a beaten man, beaten in body and spirit and tacked up on a cross to die.

Even the Bible does not give us just one picture but five—Matthew's, Mark's, Luke's, John's, and Paul's—which may be God's way of reminding us that there is always more than one way of looking at things, even something as important as what we look at on Good Friday. Matthew's and Mark's stories are almost identical, and they both agree that Jesus' last and only words from the cross were those that still send shudders through those of us who truly hear them: "My God, my God, why have you forsaken me?"

Luke tells a different story. In his account, Jesus says a good deal more from the cross, asking first that God forgive those who are putting him to death because they do not know what they are doing. Then he endures an argument between the two thieves hanging on either side of him and assures one of them that he will see paradise before the day is over. After giving a loud cry, Luke says, Jesus' last words from the cross are, "Father, into your hands I commend my spirit."

John's account, which we hear today, is the briefest. From Pilate's headquarters to the Place of the Skull, Jesus is entirely in control. No one else helps him carry his cross. He does not stumble. The women of Jerusalem do not weep for him here as they do in Luke. Giving directions even from the cross, he commends his mother Mary and his beloved disciple to each other's care and—after wetting his lips on the wine-soaked sponge held up to him—he says simply, "It is finished," and gives up his spirit. He gives it up, John says, just as he gives up his life. Nothing is taken from Jesus in John's telling of the story.

Then there is Paul, who was not a storyteller but a theologian, the first to interpret what happened on Good Friday for the church. When we were dead in our trespasses, he writes in his Letter to the Colossians, God made us alive together with Christ. God erased the record that stood against us with its legal demands. "He set this aside, nailing it to the cross" (2:14).

From these five accounts have come a world of interpretations: theologies, novels, poems, and plays; hymns, spirituals, and elaborate musical scores for voice and orchestra; movies as classical as *The Robe* and as controversial as *The Last Temptation of Christ*, not to mention twenty centuries' worth of religious art, in which painters and sculptors have looked at the cross and seen Christ not only as a first-century Jew but also as a Roman emperor, a white European, a black African, an Oriental samurai, and a Latin American freedom fighter, whose cross stands in the middle of French hillsides, Spanish bullrings, medieval cities, and Mexican barrios—some of them so realistic that it is possible to count the thorns on Christ's crown, and some of them so abstract that only their shape gives them away.

I will be speaking about some of those artists today, because all of them, in their own times and places, did what we are doing today. They regarded the cross and recorded what they saw for us, coming up with images as different from each other as they can be. No two of them are the same, but what all of them have in common is their attempt to answer the questions that Good Friday raises for us all, namely: Was the man hanging on the cross a victor or a victim? How did he understand what was happening to him? In what sense was it the will of God? And what response are we called to make?

While there may be accepted theological answers to each of those questions, the existential ones are harder to find—so hard, in fact, that for five hundred years after Christ's death on the cross there were no paintings, no drawings, no carvings of it at all. It was too confusing an event—too shocking for those who believed and too easily made fun of by those who did not. As far as anyone knows, the earliest image of the crucifixion was a piece of graffiti scratched on the wall of an ancient Roman ruin which showed a man looking up at a donkey hanging on a cross. The inscription underneath it read, "Alexamenos worships god." Elsewhere on the wall, in a different, smaller hand, a second inscription was found. "Alexamenos is faithful," it said.

The crucifixion was a baffling, embarrassing event for early Christians, who could not explain to themselves or to anyone else how the son of God wound up nailed on a cross between two thieves. So they kept the story to themselves, a family secret, until early in the fourth century the emperor Constantine saw Christ's cross in the sky and promptly won a major battle. He became a Christian on the spot and ordered the Roman Empire to follow suit, so that the cross soon became a symbol not of private defeat but of imperial victory.

The crucifixion was a baffling, embarrassing event for early Christians.

Slowly but surely, very stiff, very formal works of art began to appear showing Christ upon the cross: a stocky, beardless young man in no apparent pain, perfectly erect with his head up and his eyes open as if he were spreading his arms to welcome a guest instead of to meet his own death. They were theologically correct images, in which the divine son of God faced his death with majesty, but there was very little humanity in them. Even the figures who stood below the cross—typically, Mary the mother of God, and John the beloved disciple—even their faces were masks, showing neither grief nor gladness.

But what was an artist to do? How in the world do you portray someone who was fully human and fully divine, nailed to a cross where he suffered beyond believing and yet somehow triumphed there, so that his death was at one and the same time the worst death ever and the last? What kind of expression should you put on a face like that? What kind of language should a body like that speak? Whatever those early Christians believed then and whatever we believe now, the central problem remains: that the only son of God was convicted and sentenced to die on a cross—to die painfully and shamefully, mocked and rejected by his own people; to die young, before his ministry had even gotten off the ground; and above all to die forsaken, according to at least two accounts—to die unsure even in his own mind what it had all been about. How can you explain something like that, much less defend it? People have tried for thousands of years and still it remains an essential mystery, the deadly circumstances under which God chose to work a miracle of unprecedented life. It is not something that anyone can understand, not fully. It is something we are simply asked to accept, as Jesus himself seems to have accepted the events of Good Friday without knowing why.

He was, by *all* accounts, willing to submit himself to the unknown, willing to live out what seemed to be his destiny without having to understand it, and that is what *every* crucifixion shows: a man, suspected by many to be the son of God, dying like any son of man and woman when he had a hundred opportunities to do otherwise. Why? God knows. All the rest of us can do is watch. All the rest of us can do is stand around the cross and marvel at someone who could step into the darkness with no guarantees, trusting the promises of his God in the face of monumental contradictions, and inviting us to follow.

> *He was, by all accounts, willing to submit himself to the unknown, willing to live out what seemed to be his destiny without having to understand it.*

Because if our turns have not yet come, they will—our own turns to submit ourselves to the unknown, to step into the darkness without understanding what it is all about. We may not go bravely or wisely or compassionately; some of us may have to crawl, and others of us to be carried, but that we can go at all has everything to do with this day and this cross and this son-of-God-man, who dares us to believe that God is at the bottom of everything, especially the things we cannot understand, with strong arms waiting to catch us when all our nets break, with loving arms to cradle us when all our dying is done.

For thousands of years, Christians have sat just as we sit on this day—this Good Friday, this Dreadful Friday—and they have stared at the cross, which no one has ever fully understood, but in which each of us is asked to believe. It goes without saying that in order to do so we must be willing not to know everything, but to believe that God does, and that everything, finally, will be all right.

On her deathbed almost six hundred years ago, Dame Julian of Norwich received a series of visits from her crucified Lord. He stood at the foot of her bed and consoled her, saying, "All shall be well, and all shall be well, and all manner of thing shall be well."

That is, in the end, the message that the cross calls us to believe without knowing how or why: that come hell and high water; come affliction and hardship, persecution, hunger, nakedness, peril and sword; come whatever may, nothing can separate us from the love of God in Jesus Christ our Lord, who has promised us that everything, finally, shall be well. Amen.

Chapter Sixteen

Someone to Blame

John 19:8-11a

ACCORDING TO TRADITION, PONTIUS Pilate is the villain of Good Friday, the Roman governor of Jerusalem who had the power to pardon Jesus but who failed to do so. Every time we recite the Nicene Creed we name him as the one under whom our Lord was crucified, and he, along with the two Herods, has gone down in history as a mortal enemy of the faith.

But a close reading of the story gives a different picture. It is all Pilate can do to keep up with Jesus, who keeps turning the tables into the governor's shins until it is difficult to tell just who is the interrogator and who is the interrogatee. Answering Pilate's questions with his own, Jesus transforms their encounter into a mystical debate on the nature of kingship, authority, and truth—until Pilate is so confused that he does not know what to think or do. Three different times he goes out to the crowd to tell them that he can find no case against Jesus, and three different times they demand the death sentence.

Finally, torn between public pressure and the verdict of his own heart, Pilate hands Jesus over to be crucified, but only after Jesus has, in effect, pardoned him, by assuring him that he acts not under his own authority but under the authority of God. It is Jesus' way of telling him—and telling us—that what is about to happen is the will of God, not the will of Pilate nor of the crowd nor of the world.

Certainly, that is the church's traditional teaching on the subject of Good Friday—that by his obedience on the cross, Jesus freed us from the power of sin and reconciled us to God. He canceled our bond, Paul writes in Colossians, he paid our bail. He raised us from the dead by dying himself, and made the whole creation new. As a theological statement, that is something we may believe without being able to explain it. We may take it on faith, but try teaching it to a child. "Jesus was the son of God, see. God was his father, and God loved the world so much that he sent Jesus to die on the cross for our sins, because someone had to pay for all the bad things we had done and God decided. . . ."

"Wait just a minute," that child will say. "You mean to tell me that God killed his own son? Why would he do a thing like that? What kind of father is he, anyway?"

In his book *Messengers of God*, Holocaust survivor Elie Wiesel talks about the difference between Judaism and Christianity by comparing the two mountains that rise high in each one. For Judaism, it is Mount Moriah, where Abraham bound his son Isaac, his only son Isaac, whom he loved, and laid him on a bed of kindling wood. For Christianity the mountain is Golgotha, where, according to tradition, another father bound another only son to a deadly piece of wood. The difference between the two religions, Wiesel says, is that in the Jewish story the father does *not* kill the son, but in the Christian story he does, founding a religion that has gone on to use death as a means of glorifying God through centuries of inquisitions and holy wars. "For the Jew," Wiesel says, "all truth must spring from life, never from death."[1]

Whether you agree with him or not, he has a point. It is very difficult to reconcile a God of love with a God who wills a child's death, for whatever reason. How do you relate to a parent like that? I will tell you how: cautiously, if not fearfully. If God would do that to Jesus, whom God loved, what in the world might happen to those of us who have nothing at all to recommend us? And even if we had, wouldn't that be bad news too? Isn't the deep down message of the cross that if you are really good, like Jesus, you will die?

> *It is very difficult to reconcile a God of love with a God who wills a child's death, for whatever reason.*

The earliest surviving picture of the crucifixion is a carved ivory tablet from northern Italy, made sometime between A.D. 420 and 430.

It shows five figures, all short and stocky, their faces all but rubbed away by time. From right to left, they appear to be a Roman soldier, Christ on the cross, John the beloved disciple, Mary the mother of God, and right behind her, his limp hand brushing her elbow, Judas hanging from a tree, with his blood money scattered on the ground beneath his feet. He is clearly the villain in the scene, who has received his just reward, but in later crucifixion scenes it is more difficult to tell who is at fault. The major players are all gone, for one thing. John is the only disciple in sight, and no one from the Jewish or Roman governments is there—just some women and some soldiers and a few passersby.

In one classic arrangement, Jesus' friends are placed on his right side—his mother is there, and the beloved disciple, along with the converted centurion and the thief who repented. His enemies are placed on his left—the soldiers, the chief priests, the unrepentant thief. But none of them actually killed Jesus, unless you count the unlucky one whose job it was to hammer the nails. It is hard to say exactly who did. Was it Judas, who sold privileged information to the chief priests so that they knew where to arrest Jesus? Or was it Annas, who turned Jesus over to Caiaphas the high priest? Or was it Caiaphas, who turned Jesus over to Pilate because Jewish law forbade him to put Jesus to death himself? Was it the mob, who chose to pardon Barabbas instead of Jesus, or was it Pilate, who gave in to public pressure and handed Jesus over to be crucified? Or was it the soldiers themselves, who carried out the death sentence and then squabbled over Jesus' clothes?

Pick one. Pick any one of them and you have still not solved the crime, which is as complicated as any murder mystery ever written. It is as hard as deciding who is to blame for any crime reported in the morning paper. Sure, the close-faced man in the mug shot is the one who did it, but who else is to blame? How about the mother or father who abused him before he could walk, or the teacher who graduated him when he could not write his name, or the bootlegger who sold him grain alcohol when he was twelve, or the pusher who introduced him to crack, or the judge who sent him to jail instead of to treatment, or the parole officer who misplaced his file?

Ask questions like these and it begins to sound as if the whole fallen creation is to blame, as if the real enemy—past, present, and future—

is everything in this world that is set against God. Like Judas and the mob, the enemy in us wants to deal with our disappointment by betraying those who have let us down. Like Annas and Caiaphas, the enemy in us wants to deal with our fear by condemning those who threaten us. Like Pilate, the enemy in us wants to deal with public pressure by throwing up our hands; and like the soldiers, the enemy in us wants to deal with the call to personal responsibility by just following orders. *Whose* will put Jesus on the cross? Was it God's? Or was it our own?

In a sense, of course, it was inevitable. His death was as easy to foresee as that of a lamb grazing among wolves, except that it was more conscious than that. It was not that Jesus was incapable of defending himself. He could have stopped his teaching, or at least compromised on it. He could have exercised his privilege as the son of God, or he could have faded into the woodwork, blending into the crowd like any other Galilean while the soldiers mistook someone else for Jesus.

It was not that he could not save himself, but that he *would* not save himself, because that was not who he was. If anything, he was put to death for being completely who he was and for refusing to be less than who he was, which so offended the whole fallen creation that it conspired to wipe him off the face of the earth and did.

> It was not that he could not save himself, but that he would not save himself, because that was not who he was.

One interpretation of the Abraham and Isaac story I mentioned a moment ago is that it was a story about Abraham's love of God and what it was based on. By asking Abraham to sacrifice his only son, God asked him if he was willing to give up what he loved most: if he was willing to give up his son and a ripe old age surrounded by his grandchildren and great-grandchildren; if he was willing to give up his bright future as the patriarch of a people as numerous as the stars in the sky. He asked Abraham, in short, if he was willing to give up all the benefits of his faith for the singular love of God.

However cruel a bargain it may sound to us, Abraham was willing to do so, and in the end he did not have to. A ram appeared, caught in a thicket, and Abraham sacrificed it in place of his son. Likewise, in the story at hand, Jesus was willing to give up all the benefits of his faith and he did not have to do so either, but he did. For the singular love of God he gave everything he had to give—refusing to back down on his good news about what that love might mean for the world, even if it cost him his life.

But if we are to draw the final parallel between the first story and the second one, Jesus does not equal Abraham the father, nor does he equal Isaac the son. Jesus equals the ram, who in some way far, far beyond our understanding became the sacrifice so that all the sons and daughters of Abraham might go free, and so that every participant in that drama on Good Friday—Judas, Annas, Caiaphas, Pilate, the mob, the soldiers, the chief priests, and scribes—all of them went home free and forgiven too.

> *Jesus equals the ram, who in some way far, far beyond our understanding became the sacrifice so that all the sons and daughters of Abraham might go free.*

Whose will put Jesus on the cross? God knows. But there is a distinct possibility that it was Jesus' own magnificent will, by which he offered himself to us then and offers himself to us still—a gift, a pardon, a release, a sacrifice, a meal—not to satisfy some cosmic bookkeeper in the sky but to leave no doubt about his feelings for us. By upending the cup that was handed to him, he made sure that wherever we go in this life and whatever happens to us, we have a companion who has been there before us, who has done ferocious battle with all the powers of darkness that try to separate us from God and from one another and *who has won*. Amen.

Chapter Seventeen

The Triumphant Victim

John 19:28-30

AMONG THE MANY THINGS THAT Christians have argued about over the years is the question of exactly how Christ's human and divine natures fit together. Did he know everything that would happen to him in his life, and did he know how he would die? Or was he more like us? Did he wake up every morning wondering what God had in store for him that day and praying that he would be equal to the task?

I suppose that the only people who have struggled with this question as hard as the theologians have are the artists who dare to portray Christ—especially Christ on the cross—and who must decide what to show there. Should the eyes show confidence or bewilderment? Should they look up to heaven or be cast down to earth? Should the head be held high and defiant or should it fall to one side, heavy with the weight of the world? Should the hands be clenched or open? Should the body be that of someone in his prime or the husk of a man about to cast off his fetters and fly?

Over the centuries, those who have portrayed Christ in paint, metal, wood, or stone have answered those questions in every conceivable way. From the first crucifixion scene carved into ivory fifteen hundred years ago to the crystal crucifix of a female Christ commissioned for the Cathedral of Saint John the Divine in New York, artists have walked around and around the cross and have seen something new each time. But there have been definite trends in their visions, and to watch their work change from age to age and place to place is like watching a visual journal of how our own ideas have changed about who Christ was and is and what he means to us.

The earliest images of the crucifixion were very formal, very stylized tableaux, reigned over by a Christ who was clearly a king. The church was still young, remember, and defending itself against all kinds of foes. There was no sense advertising a God who looked like a loser, so those Romanesque and Byzantine artists showed the world a winner instead. Fully clothed, with a real crown on his head, Christ looks out at you with his eyes wide open and his face at peace. His body does not so much hang from the cross as stand suspended in front of it. If his feet are nailed down at all they are nailed apart, so that his figure is perfectly erect. When he is shown with the two thieves, his cross is significantly higher than theirs. He is the highest thing around, and therefore the closest to God.

But then something happened. Perhaps because those early artists paid so much attention to Christ's divinity, the Gothic artists who followed them attended to his humanity, showing a Christ on the cross who has been beaten to death. With his eyes closed and his head held so low that it is often impossible to see his face, he hangs all but naked on the cross, his only crown a crown of thorns. His feet are nailed together so that his whole body twists to the side, and his arms are bent at such an angle that it is a wonder they do not break. Whereas the earlier Christ was raised high up in the sky, this Christ hangs much closer to the earth. He is no longer a royal banner to be saluted but a very fleshy, very real Lord to be suffered *with*. It is not possible to watch him from a distance. To witness the scene of his death is to participate in it, and to be changed by it forever.

> *Whereas the earlier Christ was raised high up in the sky, this Christ hangs much closer to the earth.*

That was the Christ of the late Middle Ages, portrayed by artists who took seriously not only his humanity but also their own sin. The salvation they represented did not come cheap; Christ's agony on the cross made the cost clear. But then along came the Renaissance, and again things changed. Human achievement in the arts and sciences seemed so much a reflection of the God in us that Christ's two natures drew closer together than ever before. In the crucifixion scenes of the fifteenth and sixteenth centuries he is definitely a *human* on the cross, but a *divine* human, who suffers death heroically and whose body remains beautiful even after his death. Angels crowd the air around him, catching drops of his blood in gold and silver chalices and waiting to escort his soul home. The setting for the crucifixion is no longer limited to Jerusalem. This Renaissance Christ is painted in front of classical European cities and elaborate landscapes. He can be found anywhere, but while his portraits show supreme artistic merit, they show very little human feeling. The crucifixion has become an exquisite work of art, and not the baffling work of God.

Throughout the next several centuries, these same themes repeated themselves, asking the same questions over and over again and answering them in different ways. How much God was there in Christ and how much human? Did he understand what was happening to him on the cross or did he not? Was he a victim or a victor?

Theologically, I suppose, you could say he was both. He was a victim in that his death involved incredible suffering and shame, neither of which you would expect God to undergo. He was stripped naked in public, beaten with strips of leather studded with nails until the muscles in his back were laid bare, and then dressed in royal robes and made fun of, before being made to carry his own cross to the place where he was executed as a criminal. He was totally misunderstood and outnumbered, deserted by his friends and tortured by his enemies. He was a victim in that he set the existing record for voluntary humiliation.

But he was a victor in that his submission was finally not to his persecutors but to his own will. His life was not taken from him. He gave it, laying it down for his friends and for the whole world in an act of self-sacrifice that we remember today. So theologically speaking, I guess you could say he was both victim and victor.

But humanly speaking the answer goes deeper. Pain may be the biggest test of faith that any of us is ever called to face. Physicians tell us that pain is a good thing because it warns us to retreat—to drop the hot pan, get off the broken glass, stay away from the cat's sharp claws. Pain is our warning that something is dangerous to us. It is our warning to do an about-face and head in the opposite direction, and that goes for emotional as well as physical pain. Jesus, however, did not seem to get the message. Contrary to all good advice and common sense, he willingly entered into pain, refusing to be controlled by it and riding it out all the way to the end.

> *Pain may be the biggest test of faith that any of us is ever called to face.*

In the fourteenth century, Saint Bridget of Sweden had a vision in which the blessed virgin Mary described her son's death in this way:

> "When my Son saw me standing with His friends at the foot of the Cross, He cried out to His father in a loud distressed voice, 'My Father, why has thou forsaken me?' As if He said, 'Only you, my Father, can now take pity on me.' Then His eyes became half-dead, His teeth covered in blood, His face drawn, His mouth open, and His tongue dripping blood. So dried up was His body, that His chest seemed glued to His back, as if He had no entrails. All the rest was pale from the immense loss of blood. . . . With the approach of death the immense pain broke my Son's heart. His limbs contracted and His head was slightly raised and then fell back. Through His open mouth you could see the tongue red with blood. His hands tore themselves away a little from their nails so that all His weight was on the feet. His fingers and arms became distended and His back pressed firmly against the Cross."[1]

He was, humanly speaking, a victim, who was robbed on Good Friday of all that he might have been and done for the world and who was hurt to death. But he was also, humanly speaking, a victor, who never surrendered the total integrity that was his only real crime. From beginning to end, he was exactly who he said he was. Like a musical note so high and clear that it shattered everything around him, his sense of himself and of his God was more real than anything else on that hill outside Jerusalem, so real that even pain and the threat of death could not obscure it. He was a victor because he was able to trust in God's promises to him when all the evidence stood against them, and because he would not back down on the message he was born to bring: that God is in love with the world, that God has a major investment in flesh and blood, and that God is partial toward those who find themselves at the end of the line and the bottom of the heap. Jesus might have mumbled that last part and saved his life, but he declined to take it back and the rest is history. He died on the cross, a victim and a victor, the crucified, despised, beloved son of God in whom God was well pleased.

Modern works of art on the subject run the gamut; contemporary images of the crucifixion come with Christs in every color, against every background. In Africa he is a tribal chief with full ebony lips; in China he is an Oriental sage with a drooping moustache; in Nicaragua he is a peasant farmer, hanging on a cross in his work clothes in the middle of his field. Picasso painted him in a Spanish bullring, while the French painter Rouault shows him as the friend of factory workers, prostitutes, and dying soldiers. Marc Chagall, a Russian Jew, painted over twenty crucifixion scenes during his lifetime—many of them during the Second World War—in which Jesus clearly stands for the suffering of Jews everywhere.

For all of these artists, who are preachers in their own right, Jesus is the face of God who is encountered in everyday life, wherever the brokenness of the world can no longer be ignored. He is the incomprehensible love of God come to live among the poor and despicable, the Lord who cannot show them the human side of his divinity without showing them also the divine side of their own humanity. He is the wounded healer who turns the expectations of the world upside down, making glory out of humiliation, making victory out of defeat, making life out of death.

> *Jesus is the face of God who is encountered in everyday life, wherever the brokenness of the world can no longer be ignored.*

In some of the oldest crucifixion scenes we have, his cross is shown to be a green, living thing, with fresh branches sprouting out of it and tender young leaves springing forth. It is, of course, not the killing tree but the tree of life from the garden of Eden, and Jesus is the sweet, ripe first fruit of it.

In the Church of the Holy Sepulchre in Jerusalem, you have to climb a steep flight of stairs to reach the Chapel of the Crucifixion. Everything is gold and silver there, with the flames of a hundred candles bouncing off every gleaming surface. Pilgrims from around the world stand in line to crawl under the stone altar and place their hands in the gold-rimmed hole where the cross stood. When you go back down the stairs, you can see a second chapel directly underneath the first, only this one is completely unadorned—just a rock behind a metal grill door, the base of the stone upon which the cross was planted.

But ask someone who knows and you will find out that it is, according to legend, the place where Adam was buried, and the place where he was both baptized and redeemed as well, when the water and blood from Christ's body flowed down from above on Good Friday. On that day, Adam's sin was canceled, his curse reversed, and the whole creation was made new.

"Were you there when they crucified my Lord?" Many of us find that hymn running through our heads on Good Friday because that is, after all, what this day is about: it is about being there, about watching the cross and wondering what in the world it all means. During the Vietnam war, I am told, other verses were added to the song, verses like, "Were you there when they burned a land with bombs?" or "Were you there when they turned away the poor?"—the point being, I suppose, that it is not only a matter of where we would have been had we been there that long, long time ago, but where we are now, in a world where chaos still reigns and where all the forces that rebel against God are still building and filling their quota of crosses, both visible and invisible.

"Were you there when they crucified my Lord?" Where are you now, in relationship to the cross? What do you make of it, what does it make of you, what do you think, feel, wonder, hope, fear, *know?* Because no theology, no work of art, no choral passion or catechism can finally make sense out of it all for you or for me. Our job, on Good Friday, is simply to sit here, to stand here, to kneel here before this cross and to enter into our own living encounter with it—with this instrument of death, this tree of life, this living, dying Lord—so that when all is said and done, it is we, good friends in Christ, it is we ourselves who are the living, breathing explanation of it all, the ongoing interpreters of what he means to this world in which we live—the world in which, for love, he died. Amen.

Chapter Eighteen

The Myth of Redemptive Violence

John 19:14-16

"ALL SORROWS CAN BE BORNE," SAYS THE writer Isak Dinesen, "if you put them into a story or tell a story about them." On Good Friday we hear the familiar but no less painful story of Jesus' betrayal, arrest, rejection, beating, interrogation, condemnation, and death. Any one of those sorrows is enough to make your heart cramp, but by putting them all together in one story John (or should I say God?) has given us a way to sit through them, at least. Some of us have heard the story fifty times or more. We know when to brace ourselves, and whom to watch out for. We even have favorite parts, if that is the right word—places where the story comes so close to our own stories that we know how true it is, even when the truth is awful.

Maybe that is what Dinesen was talking about. There is a strange kind of comfort in a story that tells the absolute truth about how bad things can get—that spares no details and takes no prisoners. You can trust a story like that a whole lot better than you can trust one that has been all prettied up. Plus, the very fact that someone is telling it means that you are not alone. Someone else has been there. Someone else knows what it is like, and that company—that communion—can make all the difference.

> *There is a strange kind of comfort in a story that tells the absolute truth about how bad things can get.*

The thing about this story is that there are so many parts to play, and there is only one good guy in the whole bunch. All the rest conspired to do him in, either consciously or unconsciously—some of them by being weak and others by being cruel, some of them by being apathetic and others by being zealous. They are all human, in other words. The story tells us the truth about that too. To be human is not only to know Jesus' side of the story but to know Judas's side as well. And Peter's, and Caiaphas's, and Pilate's, and the crowd's. They are all inside of us somewhere, whether they are hidden or exposed, pushed down or pushing back. We are not proud of them, but there they are, reminding us that this story did not just happen once upon a time.

It has happened every day since then, and it is still happening right now, as Jesus goes on dying to show us another way to live. Let me tell you what I mean. In his book *Engaging the Powers*, Bible teacher Walter Wink talks about something he calls the myth of redemptive violence.[1] The basic idea, he says, is as old as the Babylonian religion that pre-dated Judaism. According to that faith, the world was created when Marduk, the god of Babylon, killed his mother Tiamat, the goddess of the ocean. With her death, chaos was tamed. Marduk created the cosmos from her dead body, and the king of Babylon became Marduk's representative on earth. The king's job was to maintain order. He was entrusted with keeping the peace, and whenever things got out of hand, he simply imitated his namesake Marduk by crushing the opposition. Violence was his divine right. It was how the world was made, and it was the only thing strong enough to keep chaos at bay.

We can act as if we are horrified by this if we want to, but it is how we live every day. The average American child watches 36,000 hours of television by the time he or she is eighteen, including some 15,000 murders. Some of these murders are committed by villains, but just as many are carried out by superheroes. From Popeye to Batman to

Teenage Mutant Ninja Turtles, we have taught our children that violence is bad only if the bad guys do it. If the good guys do it, then everyone is allowed to cheer. Or, in the words of Dick Tracy, "Violence is golden when it is used to put evil down."

This, Wink says, is the myth of redemptive violence—that the only way the world can be saved is to get the weapons out of the hands of the hoodlums and into the hands of the righteous, who can be trusted to hurt bad guys only and whom God will pardon for the blood they spill. Think Clint Eastwood, Arnold Schwarzenegger, Bruce Willis. Every weekend, people turn over millions of dollars in cash for the pleasure of watching these superheroes redeem the world with their guns and fists and sophisticated explosives. The arch villain is pumped full of bullets, and everyone in the audience feels safer for a moment. The myth of redemptive violence.

It is exactly what is going on in today's story. While it is hard for us to grasp, Jesus was a villain for large numbers of people. For the guardians of the law, he was an outlaw who seemed to think that his own understanding of things was superior to a judicial system that had evolved over hundreds of years. For the defenders of the faith, he was a heretic, who took outrageous liberties in the name of God. His only real fans were the common people, who saw in him someone who might free them from the heavy hands of the priests and the police. Yet even they made him a villain in the end, because he would not come on strong enough. They wanted a revolution. Jesus wanted something else, which he could never fully explain to them. His kingdom was not of this world, he told them. Fine, they replied. Let him move on to the next world, the sooner the better. Barabbas was more their type anyway. At least he had the guts to fight back.

In this way, everyone involved agreed that Jesus should be put to death. It suited the people, who had no use for a pacifist king. It suited the Romans, who welcomed any opportunity to subdue the Jews. A public execution during Passover was an excellent way to remind the children of Israel who was really in charge. It suited the high priests, whom Rome held responsible for the behavior of the people. Better they should find a way to kill this one man than to let him go on stirring everyone up so that Rome killed hundreds more of them. His death made perfect sense all the way around. It was the best, the only way, to redeem the situation. Kill the troublemaker and the trouble will go away. The myth of redemptive violence.

It is the myth by which we live, even if we have never been involved in condemning someone to death. We spank our children to teach them respect. We arm ourselves to keep the peace. We kill people who kill people to show them that killing people is wrong. We are fascinated by vigilantes like Bernard Goetz, who cut through the red tape of the courts by shooting muggers right on the spot. We support diplomacy up to a point, but no handshake with the enemy cheers our hearts like the sight of victorious troops coming home.

We are collaborators in the myth of redemptive violence, even if all we do is sit and watch. When bad gets worse, we really do believe that the way to fight fire is with fire, and this scorched earth of ours has taught us nothing. Meanwhile, Jesus hangs on the cross, stubbornly refusing to fight at all. He has taken into himself all the violence flung against him and he will not give it back. Abused, he will not abuse. Condemned, he will not condemn. Abandoned, he remains faithful. By choosing to die rather than to retaliate, he disarms the bomb of redemptive violence, wrapping himself around it to protect the rest of us from it. It kills him in the process, but that is how we know he won. The violence stopped with him. It caused his death, but it got none of his life. His life belonged to God, who sent him to show us another way to live.

Day by day, he invites us to follow him—not Marduk, not Batman, not Caiaphas or Pilate, but him—the one who would not resort to violence, not even to save his own life—the one who fought back by refusing to fight back and who replaced the myth of redemptive violence with the truth of indestructible love. Here, then, is another way to redeem the world: not by killing off the troublemakers but by dying to violence once and for all. Because he did, we can. He died to show us how. We live to show him we got the message.

"All sorrows can be borne, if you put them into a story or tell a story about them." This is a sorrowful story, all the way around. It is also the story of a cosmic success. Whether the world receives it as such remains to be seen. Amen.

Chapter Nineteen

The Silence of God

John 19:37

THIS IS WHAT WE DO ON GOOD FRIDAY. We gather to look at the wreckage of the cross—or should I say the wreckage on the cross—just look at it for an hour or two, as rapt as any crowd that stands around a bad accident, transfixed by our nearness to tragedy.

"Is he dead?"

"I don't know. I can't see."

"There's so much blood. He's got to be."

Only this is no stranger. This is our own flesh and blood—God's own flesh and blood—the one we pray to, the one with power to heal, to cast out demons, to raise people from the dead—dying himself now, as helpless as a kitten. It is all he can do to hold up his head. Everything else is tacked down now, nailed firmly in place. He cannot wipe the blood from his temples. He cannot cover his nakedness. The rescuer, unrescued. The savior, unsaved.

What can it mean, that he should die this way? Our fondest hopes die with him this day: that the omnipotent God will protect those who believe in him, that those who find favor with God will be spared fear, pain, loss, abandonment. That is what we wish. It is even what we pray. But on Good Friday we learn that it simply is not true. Here

---

Chapters 19, 20, and 21 were preached on the same day during a traditional three-hour Good Friday service.

is God's chosen one, God's beloved, as forsaken as any heretic. Friends gone. Future gone. God gone, for all he can tell, him with no more than three hours' breath left in his cup.

> Here is God's chosen one, God's beloved, as forsaken as any heretic.

As awful as it is, I will tell you something more shocking: there are people who say that Good Friday means more to them than Easter does. They have nothing against the lilies, the trumpets, the lovely children. It is just that Good Friday, as awful as it is, is more recognizable to them. They know about suffering. They know about death. They know their way around this wreckage, and there is some sort of comfort in the fact that God knows it too. Easter is hard to believe. Good Friday is not hard to believe. We live in the land at the foot of the cross.

It is too bad that John's Gospel is the one we are given on Good Friday. It is so cleaned up and brave. No agony in the garden, no stumbling on the way, no cry from the cross. Jesus is fully in charge of his own execution. He identifies himself to his captors. He debates Pilate brilliantly and carries his own cross to Golgotha all by himself. Then, mounted upon it in no apparent pain, he arranges for the care of his mother. He himself needs nothing. When he says, "I am thirsty," John lets us know it is not because he is really thirsty. It is in order to fulfill the scripture. Once that has been handled, it is all over and Jesus says so. Not "Father, forgive them for they know not what they do." Not "Why have you forsaken me?" But "It is finished," and it is. He bows his head and gives up his spirit. Gives it up. No one takes it from him. He is in charge from beginning to end.

Maybe that is the gospel we are given today because someone thought it might help us a little, to have such a strong and fearless savior. He is nobody's victim. He is God's own martyr, who goes to his death with all the eagerness of a bride. And it does help me, to believe in that kind of courage. I have read about it in other times and places: civil rights workers going down under the fire hoses, Archbishop Romero gunned down at the altar, the Yugoslavian cellist who placed his folding chair in the street in Sarajevo—right in the path of sniper fire—and played Albinoni's adagio in memory of the dead.

My heart melts at courage like that, only I suspect it is beyond me. If I have any courage in me at all, it is another kind. Not John's kind, but Mark's kind, the one we hear on Palm Sunday. In that Gospel, Jesus' suffering on the cross ends with a cry of total dereliction. Having begged God for a way out, he receives no answer and dies abandoned to the sick jokes of hostile strangers. His courage is not the courage of a conquering savior. It is, instead, the courage of a beaten and bewildered man who goes on believing in God although God is nowhere to be found.

All of us have heard plenty about Christ's physical suffering on the cross—the scourge, the nails, the thorns, the spear. Recently I heard someone add to that list the splinters that must have gouged his raw back as he slid down the timber when it was raised. This is excruciating stuff, but I have never been convinced by it. I know people whose bodily torture has gone on for years, not hours. As deforming as it can be, physical pain alone is not the agony of the cross. There is also the betrayal of intimate friends, who slept when they were needed most, who sold him to his enemies, who denied that they had ever known him. These are not nails in the hands. These are nails in the heart. And still, they are not the worst.

The worst is the utter silence of God. The God who does not act. The God who is not there. The God who—by a single word—could have made all the pain bearable but who did not speak, not so Jesus could hear, anyway. The only voice at the end was his own, screaming his last, unanswered question at the sky.

All his life he had acted and spoken like someone in on God's will and full of God's power. Twice that was confirmed by a voice from heaven. First, at his baptism. "You are my Son, the Beloved; with you I am well pleased." And again on the mount of the Transfiguration. "This is my Son, the Beloved; listen to him!" I have always wondered why it did not happen one more time, on that last day. What a difference it would have made. A confirmation like that, a blessing on the destitute moment at hand. But it did not come and Jesus died alone, having pronounced himself abandoned by God.

This is what every believer must reckon with—God's silence—not just then but also now—the same kind of silence that follows our own pleas to God to *do something*—protect us, rescue us, give us a way out. Good Friday is the day we receive no answer and must suffer that silence with the crucified one—wondering what it says about us, wondering what it says about God.

> Good Friday is the day we receive no answer and must suffer that silence with the crucified one—wondering what it says about us, wondering what it says about God.

In his book *Silence*, the Japanese writer Shusaku Endo tells the story of a seventeenth-century Portuguese missionary named Rodrigues who goes to Japan to save souls. Preparing himself for his mission, he spends a great deal of time contemplating the face of Christ, in which he sees every quality he himself wishes to possess: courage, serenity, wisdom, faith. It is an altogether noble image, only it remains just that for Rodrigues—a silent image that does not offer him either guidance or consolation. When he arrives in Japan, he is quickly in need of both.

Walking right into a national uprising against Christians, he soon finds himself in prison, where his captors order him to renounce his faith. Sustained by the brave face of Christ, he refuses, hoping to be martyred on the spot. Instead he is returned to his cell, where he listens for some word from the Lord. All he hears are the cries of his fellow prisoners—that and a strange snuffling sound that he takes to be the snoring of the guards.

When he is yanked from his cell again the next morning and refuses once again to renounce his faith, he learns that the strange sound he heard in the dark is the labored breathing of Japanese Christians. They have been crucified upside down, their heads half buried in pits of excrement. They will hang there like that, his guards tell him, until he renounces his faith. Rodrigues is paralyzed. Shall he betray the Christ or the Christians? That is his choice. If he chooses the Christ, he turns his back on the Christians. If he chooses the Christians, he turns his back on the Christ.

While he agonizes over his decision, the guards bring a metal image of Christ into the room and place it at Rodrigues' feet. They tell him to trample it, to put his foot right in the middle of it and grind it with his toe. Looking down at it, Rodrigues sees that it is already crushed and soiled by the feet of those who have gone before him. It bears no resemblance to the face he has adored all his life, the silent face to whom he has prayed his desperate prayers. Torn between his loyalty to it and his loyalty to those who are snuffling in the dark, he is hung between the two when he hears the voice of Christ, coming to him from the image at his feet. "Trample! Trample! I more than anyone know of the pain in your foot. Trample! It was to be trampled on by men that I was born into this world."[1]

The silence of God is broken. Christ speaks, not from some safe place outside human suffering but from the very heart of it. He is the trampled one, the crushed and soiled one whose loyalty to human-kind leads him to endure all that we endure—right up to and including the silence of God. When Jesus howls his last question from the cross, it is God who howls—protesting the pain, opposing it with his last breath. Only this is no defeat. This is, contrary to all appearances, a triumph over suffering. By refusing to avoid it or to lie about it in any way, the crucified one opens a way through it.

He hallows it by engaging it. He shows us how. We are not supposed to love suffering. We are allowed to hate it and to do everything in our power to bring it to an end, only we may not avoid it. That is not one of our choices. Today we look on the one whom we have pierced. More important, we listen. To the silence. To the howl. What is the gospel, in the land at the foot of the cross? When God is silent, people of faith cry out. When people of faith cry out, it is God who speaks. Amen.

Chapter Twenty

The Will of God

John 19:11

THAT GOD SHOULD WILL THE DEATH OF Jesus may be the single hardest thing we Christians are given to believe. The virgin birth, the miracles, the resurrection—these things may puzzle us. We may even decide we can get along just fine without them, but the crucifixion is not negotiable. It happened. And according to the historical faith of the church, it happened because God wanted it to. "He stretched out his arms upon the cross, and offered himself, in obedience to your will, a perfect sacrifice for the whole world."

That is how one eucharistic prayer puts it. We call it the atonement—the satisfaction—the idea being that Christ paid for our sins. We were so bad, it seems, and our crimes against God were so great, that justice demanded the sacrifice of life. The only way God could honor that demand and still preserve our lives was to find someone else to be sacrificed in our place. Jesus is who God sent—the divine self made flesh—the crucified one who set us free by taking our death sentence upon himself.

This last part is the part we hear the most about, thanking God for our pardon, but there is no getting around the detail that God killed Jesus. Theologian Dorothee Sölle calls it "sadistic theology" and wants no part of it. "The ultimate conclusion of theological sadism," she writes, "is worshipping the executioner."[1] Holocaust survivor Elie Wiesel agrees with her. Recounting the story of Abraham and Isaac, he says that the main difference between Judaism and Christianity is that on Mount Moriah, the father did not kill his son, while on Golgotha, he did.[2] And for that reason, Wiesel says, he is eternally grateful that God made him a Jew.

His comparison makes me think of an eighteenth-century tapestry that hangs in a Jesuit monastery in Germany. In it, Isaac is bound to the altar. Abraham is kneeling a little ways away, not with a knife but with a flintlock in his hand, taking aim at his only son. But the boy is perfectly safe. A plump angel floats above Abraham's head, peeing a high arc onto the firing pin of the gun. Below him, you can read the legend: "Abraham, you aim in vain. An angel sends a little rain."[3]

Where was Jesus' angel? That is what I want to know. Where was the angel with the flaming sword, to pry him loose and spirit him away? Even a voice would have done. "Stop this right now. You are about to make a terrible mistake." Only there was no voice, no angel, no interruption of the proceedings at all. As God remained silent, Jesus hung there while the life drained out of him and then he died, a young man with half his life left ahead of him. Maybe that is why we call it the will of God—simply because it happened. If God had not willed it, it would not have happened. Only that assumes a universe in which there are no other powers operating besides the power of God, and I am not so sure about that.

> *Where was Jesus' angel? That is what I want to know.*

From the very beginning, God has shared power with us, giving us power to name, to create, to choose, to act. We have done wonderful things with that privilege. We have also abused it. The dark side of our power is our power to resist God—to say no to God's yes and to thwart the divine will. We tend to dilute that fact by believing our rebellions are more or less benign, like two-year-olds pounding their parents' knees. God allows us the temporary illusion of power, we tell ourselves, but God is really in charge, and when things get bad enough God will come back into the room and set everything right.

Only what if that is not how things work? What if God has settled for limited power in order to be in partnership with us and we really can mess things up? What if God lets us? This is a different world from the first one. In the first, everything that happens, happens by the will of an all-powerful God. In this one, God's power is limited by our power to resist. What happens, happens in a world of clashing wills, so that even God is sometimes surprised.

This casts a different light on the cross. It is entirely possible that God's will for Jesus was long life and success, and that his early death was not the fulfillment of God's will but the frustration of it—the world's no to God's yes—a divine defeat. In this light, Jesus did not die to pay our bills. He died because he would not stop being who he was and who he was, was very upsetting. He turned everything upside down. He allied himself with the wrong people and insulted the right ones. He disobeyed the law. He challenged the authorities, who warned him to stop. The government officials warned him to stop. The religious leaders warned him to stop. And when he would not stop, they had him killed, because he would not stop being who he was.

> It is entirely possible that God's will for Jesus was long life and success, and that his early death was not the fulfillment of God's will but the frustration of it.

At any point along the way, he could have avoided the cross. He could have stopped operating in the open and gone underground instead. He could have stopped being such an activist and started writing books instead. He could have stopped helping other people and helped himself instead.

He could have stopped being who he was, but he did not. When the soldiers showed up in the garden to arrest him, he did not disappear into the dark. He stepped into the light of their torches and asked them whom they were looking for.

"Jesus of Nazareth," they answered him, and he said, "I am he." It is God's name in a different key, the same name God gave Moses in the burning bush. I am who I am. I will be who I will be. I am he. It was not the only possible answer. For him, maybe, but not for everyone. A little later, after Jesus had been taken to the high priest for interrogation, Simon Peter lingered in the courtyard while his teacher was being questioned. Twice someone recognized him and asked him who he was. "You are not also one of this man's disciples, are you?"

"I am not," Peter said, not once but three times. So Jesus died and Peter lived. That is the difference between "I am" and "I am not."

If Jesus had denied himself the way Peter did, he might have saved his life, but it is pretty clear he would have lost it too. Who would he have been after that? A fugitive Christ, forever on the run? Or just a pretender—someone who almost had what it took but not quite, not at the end. He could have gone on teaching, I suppose, only I doubt he could have found many students. Who shows up to learn from someone whose life mocks his teaching? Luckily for us, that is not how it happened. He had what it took. He gave all he had, opening himself up to all his life brought him.

If the cross was in any sense the defeat of God's will, then it was also the perfection of it, as one beloved human being chose to bear the consequences of being who he was and died with the same integrity he had lived. Insofar as it was the will of God that he live like that, then God's will included the possibility of his death—not as something God desired but as something God suffered.

Christianity is the only world religion that confesses a God who suffers. It is not all that popular an idea, even among Christians. We prefer a God who prevents suffering, only that is not the God we have got. What the cross teaches us is that God's power is not the power to force human choices and end human pain. It is, instead, the power to pick up the shattered pieces and make something holy out of them—not from a distance but right close up.

What the cross teaches us is that God's power is not the power to force human choices and end human pain.

By entering into the experience of the cross, God took the man-made wreckage of the world inside himself and labored with it—a long labor, almost three days—and he did not let go of it until he could transform it and return it to us as life. That is the power of a suffering God, not to prevent pain but to redeem it, by going through it with us.

Some of us like it better the other way. We would rather have a God who makes everything happen, including the cross, than a God who hangs there with us. Maybe because that allows us the hope that we can still get God to spare us.

There is a story that one day in Auschwitz a group of Jews put God on trial. They charged God with cruelty and betrayal. Forming a proper court, they appointed counselors for the prosecution and for the defense, and they heard all the arguments on both sides. At the end of the proceedings they conferred on their findings and the verdict was unanimous. The rabbi stood up to make the formal pronouncement. "This court finds God guilty as charged," he said. "Now let us go pray."

Amen.

Chapter Twenty-one

The Suffering of God

John 19:28

FOR ALL ITS PROMINENCE IN THE Christian story, suffering is a great killer of faith. Long-time believers crash into their first wall of life-threatening illness and all the light goes out of their eyes. They pack their prayer books when they go to the hospital but they do not open them once they are there. They watch television instead, cruising channels for something to busy their minds. They cannot pray. When they try, their prayers get no farther than the ceiling. One of them says he is afraid to pray now. He prayed before, and look what happened. Now all he wants to do is to lie low and try not to catch God's attention.

> *For all its prominence in the Christian story, suffering is a great killer of faith.*

Someone else is perfectly healthy, so far as she knows. It is not her own suffering that has broken her faith but the suffering of other people. She works in the emergency room of a county hospital, where she lays her hands on every kind of tragedy—the two nineteen-year-old girls killed in a car wreck, the little boy whose mother has broken his arm, the young man with AIDS whose parents say they are not taking him back home with them, that he will have to find someone else to care for him now. After a shift like this one, the doctor wants to break something. She is tired of cleaning up God's messes. If she ever believed in a loving God, she does not anymore. God is fired, for failure to act.

"Human suffering threatens all networks of meaning."[1] Some cultures are better at it than others. Those with fewer defenses against it tend to handle it better than we do. In parts of Africa, women expect to bury half their children before they are two years old. In rural China, people with cataracts go blind. In Nepal, lepers live on the steps of temples, begging alms from the faithful who pass by. On the whole, we Americans have a hard time with these scenarios, because we have the idea that they can and should be fixed.

Our mind-boggling technology and national wealth have allowed us to relieve so much suffering that we have begun to believe it should not exist at all. Where it persists, we work hard for a while. We employ experts, allocate resources. We bring all our own best values to bear and are shocked when they are not welcomed. Then—to tell the truth—most of us withdraw, walling ourselves off from those who cannot be fixed and suggesting in one way or another that it is their own damned fault. To help us feel safe from what has happened to them, we conform to an unwritten code—live in the right neighborhood, eat the right food, make good investments, be a good person—and tragedy, like a tornado, should skip right over you.

It is an illusion, of course, but a predictable one for people who do not know how to suffer. We know how to relieve suffering, and we know how to evade it. What is hard for us is to confront it, with no power to make it go away. Please do not get me wrong. The wish to end all suffering is a noble wish. It is a God-driven wish. Only there are some kinds of suffering that come with the human territory and cannot be budged. We cannot choose whether to suffer them. We can only choose how.

Suffering has been present in creation from the very beginning. As far back as the garden of Eden there was the ache of loneliness, as the first human creature longed for a partner. Then there was temptation, with all its attendant anxiety. Should we or shouldn't we? We shouldn't, but we can. We are free to choose. What will happen if we do? And of course there was the sting of finding our limits. *This tree but not that tree. Do not eat, never mind why. I am God. You are not. Remember your place in the scheme of things. I am God. You are not.*

There were more limits later on—work, pain, death—all of them results of humankind's wish to flee limits. The whole point of eating the fruit was to be like God, after all—to know everything, to live forever, never to need a thing—but what was true then remains true now: our flight from suffering perpetuates suffering. When we turn away from it in the world around us, we give it permission to spread. When we ignore it in those with whom we live, we cut ourselves off from our kinship with them. When we deny it in ourselves, we become numb to the deep parts of ourselves where both joy and sorrow live. Or worse.

Rather than confront the suffering that is part of our lives, some of us decide to search for an enemy—someone who has done this to us and who must be stopped. The Russians, the Democrats, the Hispanics, the Jews, the poor, the different, the enemy. You may have read about the Presbyterian church in Washington, D.C., that moved into a new building near the Watergate. They were delighted with their new address, where they meant to continue their soup kitchen for the homeless. Only their neighbors took one look at all those poor people and went straight to their zoning board, which voted to close down the feeding program. No one who was interviewed was against giving food to hungry people. They just did not want it done there, where they could see it.

Our flight from suffering perpetuates suffering.

In America, we are still trying to build a world in which the tragic is passé, only the tragic will not lie down and die. It keeps popping back up again, and all our efforts to avoid it simply make it worse. All things considered, it is not suffering itself, but our incapacity for suffering, that is dangerous to our health.[2] There is another way. Call it the way of confrontation. Call it the way of the cross. It is the way of those who understand that suffering is part of life—some of it to be fought and some of it to be endured—but none of it to be run from, as if running ever changed a thing.

In the 1930s, a young Jewish woman named Simone Weil applied for a one-year leave of absence from her teaching job in order to work as an unskilled laborer, first in an electrical plant and then as a machine operator for Renault. Over the objections of her family, she changed her name, rented a room near the factory, and set about living a life that was no different from that of her fellow workers. She was not a strong person, and she soon grew ill working long days for low pay. When Hitler occupied France in 1940, she worked in the resistance, finally immigrating to England where she joined the French regime in exile. As a Jew, she could not officially join the struggle for France, so she took part in it by voluntarily limiting herself to the same rations the occupied French could get with their food cards. It was all quite unnecessary. She was safe in England. She was an educated person of means, but she refused to make use of her privilege. In the spring of 1943, sick and malnourished, she entered the hospital where she died the following August at the age of thirty-four.

Why did she do it? Because she had encountered Christ and she believed him. Although she was never baptized, thinking that would make her an insider instead of an outsider like him, she believed it was possible for a person to take on suffering for the sake of others and she bet her life on it. You can read her conclusions in any number of her books. Her chief discovery was that Christian faith has nothing to do with the removal of suffering. It offers no "supernatural remedy for suffering," she wrote. What it offers, instead, is a "supernatural use for it."[3] When the soul in travail is able to go on loving God, not because life is good but simply because God is,

> if it does not renounce loving, it happens one day to hear, not a reply to the question which it cries, for there is none, but the very silence as something infinitely more full of significance than any response, like God himself speaking. It knows then that God's absence here below is the same thing as the secret presence upon earth of the God who is in heaven.[4]

I do not expect that will convince any of us to go volunteer for extra suffering as she did, but maybe it can help us confront the suffering we already have—some of it to be fought and some of it to be endured—but none of it to be run from, as if running ever changed a thing. Suffering can be a great killer of faith. It can compress the human soul into a cramped knot of pain and explode with bitterness all around. Or it can be the means by which we discover the shape of our humanity, including our kinship with God and one another. For the difference between the two, see the cross.

> *Suffering can make us indestructible, by putting us in league with the crucified one.*

That is where we learn the truth that saves our lives: suffering does not have to destroy us. It is our fear and evasion that do that. Suffering can make us indestructible, by putting us in league with the crucified one, whose own hurt battered the heart of God and broke through to abundant life. That is the promise. The cross points the way. Amen.

Chapter Twenty-two

May He Not Rest in Peace

| John 19:1-37 |

THERE WAS NO DEATH BY LETHAL INJEC-
tion in Jesus' day. There was no effort to
make capital punishment quick or humane
at all. The whole idea was to kill the convict as slowly and painfully
as possible so that everyone standing around got the message: break
the law and this could be you. The only problem was, they killed an
innocent man this time. He was no criminal. He got caught in the
bitter politics between Jerusalem and Rome, neither of which could
afford an extra king walking around. So they solved their mutual
problem by putting him to death, although each worked hard to
blame the other for his death. Whatever. It happened. He died, his
friends scattered, he was buried, and as far as I know there was never
a funeral.

Good Friday is his funeral then, our annual memorial service for
him, and I want to offer a brief eulogy. It begins with a quote from
the writer Dorothy Sayers. "It is curious," she writes, "that people
who are filled with horrified indignation whenever a cat kills a
sparrow can hear the story of the killing of God told Sunday after
Sunday and not experience any shock at all."

No, we are not in shock anymore. It is an old, old story. Love
comes into the world like a little child, fresh from God. When love
grows up, love feeds people, love heals people, love turns things
upside down. This does not sit well with the people in charge. They

warn love to leave well enough alone. Love meets hate, meets politics, meets fear. Love goes on loving, which gets love killed—not by villains in black hats but by people like us: clergy, patriots, God-fearing folk. What brought them together was their rage at him, for being less than they wanted him to be—or for being more than they wanted him to be—but in any case for not being who they wanted him to be, and they killed him for it.

He was a good man. Perhaps that is the first thing to say about him. He resisted the temptation to be more than a man, although it was clearly within his power to do so. On the whole, he limited himself to what anyone made out of flesh and blood could do, obeying the laws of gravity and mortality just like the rest of us so we could not discount our kinship with him. He did not come to put us to shame with his divinity. He came to call us into the fullness of our humanity, which was divine enough for him.

He was survived by his mother. There was no one else, although some people said there were brothers and sisters. He had no children, although he showed a real fondness for them. He called his friends "children" more than once, although he was not much older than they were. They seemed to know what he meant. He never wrote anything, except with his finger in the sand, but many of his words were remembered. You can find them easily today, printed on all sorts of things: T-shirts, coffee mugs, car bumper stickers. It is more difficult to find people who know what they mean.

He was a good man, but he was not such a good god, if being a god means being big and strong and out of reach. He was a suffering god, which no one had ever heard of before. He meant to transform the world by loving it, not by controlling it, and that made his life hell a lot of the time. Compared to the founders of other religions, he had a rough time of it. Buddha died at eighty, surrounded by his followers. Confucius died an old man too, while he was putting together the ancient writings of the Chinese people. Muhammad died in the arms of his favorite wife while he was the ruler of Arabia.

> *He was a good man, but he was not such a good god, if being a god means being big and strong and out of reach.*

Jesus was not so lucky. But if he had been luckier, what would he have had to offer all those others who die too soon—abandoned—who suffer for things they did not do, who are punished for the capital offense of loving too much, without proper respect for the authorities? His hard luck makes him our best company when we run into our own. He knows. He has been there. There is nothing that hurts us that he does not know about. On the whole, his love was not the sweet kind. It may have been sweet when he was holding a child in his arms or washing his friends' feet. But more often it was the fierce kind of love he was known for—love that would not put up with any kind of tyranny, that would not stand by and watch a leper shunned or a widow go hungry—love that turned over tables and cracked homemade whips before it would allow God to be made into one more commodity.

What else? He was a king, whether Pilate could get him to say it or not, only his kingdom was not of this world. It broke into this world from time to time—it still does—and this world could use a whole lot more of it, but we are also afraid of it. Our world is built on knowing who is up and who is down, who is in and who is out, who is last and who is first. His world turns all that upside down, and we simply cannot function like that. So we run this world our way and we make noises about wanting to do it his way, but we do not really mean it or we would.

> So we run this world our way and we make noises about wanting to do it his way, but we do not really mean it or we would.

There is this sin thing that keeps getting in our way—this fear thing, this greed thing, this broken me-me-me thing. It is not all there is to us, but it is strong stuff, and yet according to him it is finished. It has no more dominion over us, because his death killed it once and for all. You figure it out. We have been set free. His death saved us, and while no one can explain that any better than anyone can explain how he was all human and all God, it would be a terrible thing to deny. It would be like pounding in more nails. Into him. Into us.

Besides, the point is not what sense we can make of the cross but what sense the cross makes of us. We have everything to do with his death. He has everything to do with our life. God help us. Good Friday is the day for pondering these things, while Easter is still a rumor. If we are not shocked by his killing, let us at least be silenced by it. By what we have done, by what he has done, while there is still time.

> *If we are not shocked by his killing, let us at least be silenced by it.*

May he not rest in peace. May he stay busy with us, who are in grievous need of him. Amen.

Epilogue

Preaching Christ Crucified

Chapter Twenty-three

In Weakness and Much Trembling

1 Corinthians 2:1-5

ACCORDING TO MOST REPORTS, THE church as we have known it is now on the endangered species list. While faith in God has remained high in this country, faith in the church has been on a steady decline, until many of our mainline denominations are wondering how they will survive. Ask those who have stopped going to church why and you will hear a variety of answers. *Because it is boring,* they say. *Because all anyone ever talks about is money. Because I don't need any more guilt; I have a lifetime supply already.*

Add to that the highly publicized scandals of some of our better known evangelists, the current quarrel in our culture about the proper relationship between politics and religion, and you begin to understand why many observers call this the post-Christian era. We have lost our consensus about what it means to be Christian, and we have lost the language of faith we once had in common (or thought we did). I cannot think of a major denomination that currently does not have a fault line running right down the middle of it. Who can blame young people for looking elsewhere for God? Or for deciding—based on the behavior of churchgoers they know—that there is not much reason to look for God at all?

While mainline churches languish, however, a phenomenon known as the megachurch makes headlines. I recently read an article in the *New York Times* about Willow Creek Community Church near

Chicago, Illinois, which attracts more than twenty thousand people to its services on Sunday. What is their secret? They listened to unchurched people who wanted padded seats instead of pews, a live band instead of an organ, and less emphasis on threatening images like the cross. It gives some old-timers like me the willies, but it works. Who can argue with twenty thousand people?

Meanwhile, many of our denominations are responding to the crisis by putting more tools into the hands of church leaders. Almost any week of the year, I can attend a workshop on organizational management, small group dynamics, conflict resolution, or church growth. I can learn how to use business techniques like market studies, mass mailing, and telemarketing to increase church membership, and I can even get a home page on the Internet.

There is also a revival of interest in preaching, with dozens of well-attended conferences each year and a growing number of publications on preaching. Even liturgical churches, which have traditionally ranked preaching behind sacraments, are paying more attention to the role of the sermon in the life of the church. Look at what Baylor University did in 1996. They created a mini-cyclone in the world of homiletics by publishing a list of preachers in *Newsweek*, of all places.

All of these developments, and especially the last one, have given me reason to think hard about all the things we do to get people into church. Does the end justify the means, or are we playing a dangerous game with the gospel, by substituting our own expertise for the power of God?

> *Does the end justify the means, or are we playing a dangerous game with the gospel, by substituting our own expertise for the power of God?*

Take the Baylor list, for instance. On one hand, it is a great honor to be on that list. But on the other, it is a little like winding up on a billboard outside my church. I hate to think what Paul would say if he walked by and saw it. "What are you doing there, with your mug plastered all over the place? This was never supposed to be about you. Sakes alive! All twelve of you should be ashamed that anyone knows your names at all. When you get through preaching, the only name on anyone's lips should be the name of Jesus Christ."

That was the standard he held himself to, anyhow. "When I came to you," he wrote the church at Corinth, "I did not come proclaiming the mystery of God to you in lofty words or wisdom. For I decided to know nothing among you except Jesus Christ, and him crucified." He came to them in weakness and much trembling, he said. He would not dazzle them even if he could, so that their faith would rest not on his wisdom but on the power of God.

We do not know for sure what all of Paul's limitations were, but he and everyone else knew he had them. In the first place, there was that mysterious thorn in the flesh that gave him so much trouble, and in the second place, he was not all that great a preacher. He knew what some people said about him—that he was strong on paper but weak in person, with contemptible speech (2 Corinthians 10:10). According to a second-century source, *The Apocryphal Acts of Paul and Thecla*, he was "a man of small stature, with bald head and crooked legs . . . with eyebrows meeting and nose somewhat hooked."

But not all of his limits were given. This is the same Paul who founded at least seven churches and wrote thirteen eloquent letters that are quoted to this day. The book of Acts contains several of his speeches—which are anything but contemptible—along with the names of those who were converted by hearing him.

At least some of his limits, then, were chosen. Paul could impress a crowd as well as anyone could, but on the whole he held back, because as far as he was concerned, any preacher who won a following by wooing them with grand ideas and thrilling language was guilty of fraud. There was nothing exalted about Christ's life and death, he said, unless you had faith to see through them. To stand up in front of people twirling your tongue about them was to parade a fundamental misunderstanding of the gospel.

There is nothing in that gospel about being impressive or successful. There is nothing in it about being the biggest or the best at anything at all. The good news of God in Christ is that when the bottom has fallen out from under you—when you have crashed through all your safety nets and you can hear the bottom rushing up to meet you—the good news is that you cannot fall farther than God can catch you. You can't be too picky about where the catch happens, I'm afraid. Sometimes it happens after the funeral is over, as it did with Jesus, but the good news he brought back to us can never be revoked. God is stronger than death. Way past where we can see how it works, God is able to take our weakness, our fear, our trembling, and turn it into fullness of life.

Some of us get so excited about this news that we begin to think it is about us. Somewhere in the dark tunnels of our minds we turn God's power to save us into our own power to prosper and a sly kind of triumphalism slips into our theology. We look to numbers and dollars for signs of our success instead of to the holiness of our life together. We build theaters instead of churches, where religious entertainment takes the place of worship. If we are not careful, we may start to sound like spiritual big shots, who speak of God's power as if it were the power to make us healthy, wealthy, and wise when of course it is nothing of the sort. The power of God is now and has always been the power to raise us from the dead. Period. It is not about us. It is about God. Our only role is to stick our feet straight up in the air and admit that without God we might as well be put to bed with a shovel.

Now that is a message that can empty a church out fast. "Hello. It is so lovely to see you all here this evening. My message tonight will be brief and to the point. God is not in the business of protecting us from harm, and no amount of good behavior will keep us safe. For evidence of this, see the cross. Instead, God is in the business of restoring us to life, which may involve some painful procedures. If we are willing to go through it and the operation is successful, our lives will not belong to us anymore. We will be God's gifts to the world, and our 'to do' lists will have no end. If the operation is *really* successful, our good works will get us killed. P.S. Every day will be full of fresh astonishment and we will never, ever get bored."

It is not a message that sells very well, because it runs counter to most human wisdom—which is, wisely enough, about how to make it in this world. The message of the cross, on the other hand, is about how to stop trying to make it in this world and fall in love with God instead. It is about God's power, not ours, which is why Paul was so suspicious of powerful preachers.

Some of you students of the sixties may remember Marshall McLuhan's slogan, "the medium is the message," by which he meant that what someone says is only as convincing as how that person says it. Paul never read McLuhan, but he knew the same thing. To speak of Christ's painful surrender to God in loud, confident tones is a contradiction in terms. To have a garland put around your own neck for preaching about his self-sacrifice is crazy-making. Imagine, if you will, that Mother Teresa had a spokesman who was so good at what he did that he was in great demand, going from town to town eating big suppers and sleeping in fine hotels as he spoke about her work with the dying paupers of Calcutta. What is wrong with this picture?

> To speak of Christ's painful surrender to God in loud, confident tones is a contradiction in terms.

The cross is such a hard, hard piece of the gospel that most of us cannot stay converted to it for long. It is God's wisdom, after all, "secret and hidden, which God has decreed before the ages for our glory." We believe it and then we don't, popping back into the wisdom of the world, which is about success, numbers, income, prizes. Our love of this wisdom is not just a problem for preachers. It is a problem for the whole church, which is always in danger of forgetting whose spokesperson it is.

We are the lovers of a God who specializes in turning the world's values upside down. We are the followers of a Lord who waited tables and washed feet. We are the heirs of a Spirit who has power to revive the whole creation, beginning with us, but only if we will allow it—by giving up all illusions that we know how to save ourselves and begging God, one more time, to show us how it is done.

One reason we run from God's wisdom, I think, is because we do not know how to behave once we have surrendered our power. Do we just go limp now? Do we take the ads out of the newspaper, cancel the new building, hire preachers who will speak the plain truth about God with as little fanfare as possible? Probably not. We should probably go on trying to be the best we know how to be, using the best tools at hand. We just should not fool ourselves into thinking that we know what is really going on.

It is entirely possible that some of our proudest achievements are embarrassing to God, and some of our most dismal failures please God very much. There is simply no way of telling, since our wisdom is so different from God's wisdom. The only thing we can be sure of is that everything we offer up—ailing churches and prosperous ones, tongue-twirling preachers and those who struggle with every word— they are all eligible for the transforming power of God, who loves nothing better than bringing the dead back to life.

Meanwhile, the medium is the message. When we are able to give ourselves to that message without embezzling God's glory, when we are able to tell the story without cluttering it up with our own craving for success, then it becomes clearer to everyone (and especially to us) that God is the only fit object of our hearts' desires. All else is dust.

God is the only fit object of our hearts' desires. All else is dust.

"When I came to you, brothers and sisters, I did not come proclaiming the mystery of God to you in lofty words or wisdom. For I decided to know nothing among you except Jesus Christ, and him crucified." Many who came to hear Paul were disappointed by him. His speech was contemptible. He stood there trembling, with his crooked legs bumping together and his bushy eyebrows leaking sweat, as if he were afraid a lion might jump on him at any moment and tear him apart.

And you know what? Thank goodness for that. Because of that, there could be no doubt whose power was holding him up there, loosening his tongue until the words came out, and even after they came out, doing something through that short, bald man that the words themselves could not explain. It was not human wisdom on display that day, but the power of Almighty God, who is still eager to inhabit anyone who dares. Amen.

Notes

1. The Gift of Disillusionment

1. (New York: Bantam Books, 1961), 235.

4. Divine Anger

1. (New York: Simon & Schuster, 1993), 15.

16. Someone to Blame

1. Elie Wiesel, *Messengers of God: Biblical Portraits and Legends* (New York: Random House, 1976), 67.

17. The Triumphant Victim

1. Joseph Jobe, *Ecce Homo* (New York: Harper & Row, 1962), 113.

18. The Myth of Redemptive Violence

1. Walter Wink, *Engaging the Powers: Discernment and Resistance in a World of Domination* (Minneapolis: Fortress Press, 1992).

19. The Silence of God

1. Shusaku Endo, *Silence* (New York: Taplinger Publishing Company, 1979), 259.

20. The Will of God

1. Dorothee Sölle, *Suffering* (Philadelphia: Fortress Press, 1975), 28.
2. Elie Wiesel, *Messengers of God: Biblical Portraits and Legends* (New York: Random House, 1976), 67.
3. *Suffering*, 31.

21. The Suffering of God

1. William A. Beardslee et al., *Biblical Preaching on the Death of Jesus* (Nashville: Abingdon Press, 1989), 129.
2. John Douglas Hall, *God and Human Suffering: An Exercise in the Theology of the Cross* (Minneapolis: Augsburg Publishing House, 1986), 46.
3. Simone Weil, *Gravity and Grace* (New York: G. P. Putnam's Sons, 1952), 132.
4. Simone Weil, *Intimations of Christianity Among the Ancient Greeks* (Boston: Beacon Press, 1957), 199.